STOICISM

A Detailed History of Ancient Wisdom That Will Help You Cure Anxiety (The Happiness and Optimism Guide for a Good Life)

This document is geared toward providing exact and reliable information in regards to the topic and issue covered. The publication is sold with the idea that the publisher is not required to render accounting, officially permitted, or otherwise, qualified services. If advice is necessary, legal or professional, a practiced individual in the profession should be ordered.

- From a Declaration of Principles which was accepted and approved equally by a Committee of the American Bar Association and a Committee of Publishers and Associations.

The information provided herein is stated to be truthful and consistent, in that any liability, in terms of inattention or otherwise, by any usage or abuse of any policies, processes, or directions contained within is the solitary and utter responsibility of the recipient reader. Under no circumstances will any legal responsibility or blame be held against the publisher for any reparation, damages, or monetary loss due to the information herein, either directly or indirectly.

Respective authors own all copyrights not held by the publisher.

The information herein is offered for informational purposes solely and is universal as so. The presentation of the information is without contract or any type of guarantee assurance.

The trademarks that are used are without any consent, and the publication of the trademark is without permission or backing by the trademark owner. All trademarks and brands within this book are for clarifying purposes only and are the owned by the owners themselves, not affiliated with this document.

Table of Contents

INTRODUCTION AND AN IMPORTANT NOTE

Firstly, I want to thank you for purchasing this book.

I hope you enjoy this book and are able to learn more about Stoicism.

There is a lot of philosophy this book. If you do not like philosophy and want to jump to the "self-help" section of this book, you can start reading from Chapter 10 or Chapter 12.

Finally, after you are finished reading this book, will you be kind enough to leave a positive review on Amazon? I would greatly appreciate it!

CHAPTER 1: STOICISM

Stoicism is a school of philosophy that arose during the Hellenist era. It was created by a philosopher named Zeno of Citium in the year 300 BC in the ancient city of Athens. These ideas were quickly adopted by the Cynics as well as by Socrates. It caused controversial arguments among the Academics, Epicureans, and Skeptics. The word "Stoicism" comes from the Greek words Stoa Poikile (the Painted Porch), a large marketplace in the country. It was there that Stoics from different parts of the country met and conducted philosophical teachings. Soon after its creation, Stoicism spread to Rome where it blossomed.

Stoicism did not exist without criticism. Some of the emperors who reigned at the time frowned upon the philosophy. Domitian and Vespasian are two notable individuals who opposed the teachings of Stoicism in Rome. However, it greatly influenced the lives of those who tried to apply its dictates. Marcus Aurelius is one prominent adherent to the philosophy.

Stoicism positively affected many prominent philosophers throughout the ages including Spinoza, Thomas More, and Descartes. It also inspired the religion of Christianity. In the early years of this current century, Stoicism witnessed a renewal of purpose. Its teachings have become a practicable set of ideas which are related to therapies and behavior in human cognitive domains and other related fields. Stoicism preaches ethical virtues that are eudemonic in composition. It stresses that such virtues, when put into practice, are important principles to follow when humans seek happiness.

Stoics highlighted the fact that there can be "indifferents," which can either be acceptable (for instance, education, and wealth) or unacceptable (like ignorance and poverty). Humans possess the ability to plan and put virtues to good use. The philosophy of Stoicism was created to integrate its tenets into the day-to-day lives of human beings. It is based predominantly on Ethics. It is widely regarded as a branch of education that aims to explain how humans should and can live their lives.

Stoicism was influenced by what Stoics referred to as "Physics," as well as by fusion of epistemology, cognitive science, the philosophy of language, and modern Logic, which they regarded as "Logic."

HISTORICAL BACKGROUND

According to its scholars, Stoicism in the ancient world can be classified into three main stages: the Early Stoa, Middle Stoa, and the Late Stoa, which is also regarded as the Roman Imperial era.

The Early Stoa occurred between 300 BC, the days of Zeno of Citium, who created that branch of knowledge, and the days of Chrysippus, who was the third philosopher who reigned during Stoicism. The Middle Stoa stage was championed by Posidonius and Panaetius between 200 and 100 BC. The third stage is the Late Stoa or the Roman Imperial era, which lasted between 100 and 200 C.E. It was dominated by the works, teachings, and practices of notable philosophers, such as Musonius Rufus, Epictetus, Seneca, and Emperor Marcus Aurelius.

PHILOSOPHICAL ANTECEDENTS

Stoicism can be described as a Hellenist period philosophy based on eudemonia. This means it can be traced to many of its close contemporaries and antecedents. There is no doubt that Stoicism inherited some traits from the existing philosophical teachings. One of these teachings was the Socratic way of thinking, which came into existence with the help of the first set of Platonic dialogs. Platonism also emanated from the Academic School. The Peripatetic Academy also had Aristotelians. Other teachings include Epicureanism, Cynicism, and Skepticism.

It is important to note that comprehensive research into ancient records that discuss popular preachers of philosophy in the old Greco-Roman era reveals that prominent schools at that time had varied populations.

Eudemonia was widely translated to mean "a life that is worthy to live." In the modern world, its translation has been transformed to mean "happiness." Sometimes eudemonia can mean "to flourish." For many in the ancient world who believed the teachings of Stoicism, eudemonia was viewed as "being excellent in one's virtues," especially when it came to moral aspects. Although its translation was not restricted to that interpretation, it was dominantly presumed to mean as such. The idea of eudemonia is not far from the Ethics that encompass virtue. In comparison, this idea was related to the Nicomachean Ethics of Aristotle. It has also been brought back to life by philosophers such as Alasdair MacIntyre, and Philippa Foot, and others.

In many of the schools that existed around the time Stoicism was created, the distinct features helped create an understanding of what Stoicism is. For instance, in his book Euthydemus, Socrates stated that the four divisions of virtue – justice, courage, temperance, and wisdom – are the good attributes that any human being can possess. He maintained that all other attributes could not be adequately categorized as good or bad. Aristotle, on the other hand, described 12 virtues as being important for every human being. Aristotle did stress that all the virtues together could not be perfectly adequate for eudemonia. He explained that human beings had to possess a measure of education, health, attractive appearance, as well as wealth. This proves that Aristotle believed in a common-sense thought that a life full of happiness is partly dependent on the effort. While human beings can learn to restructure their characters, some conditions, such as physical and cultural constraints, can unavoidably determine the structure of human beings' lives.

The belief of the Cynics was a distinct approach during that period. While they assumed that good attributes are the divisions of virtue as outlined by Socrates, Cynics maintained that the other good attributes Aristotle mentioned could be classified as attributes that create confusion. In fact, such things are to be ignored. Like Diogenes of Sinope, Cynics were known to have a rather eclectic, ascetic way of living, as explained by Laertius (Diogenes). He related the event of a particular day when he watched a small child drink right from his palms. This led Diogenes to throw away the cup that he had attached to his bag. He professed that a child had defeated him in living plainly.

Aristotle's belief was definitive – that is, it was exclusively aristocratic in nature. The approach simply meant that as long as certain humans did not have some of life's privileges they could not experience eudemonia. Cynics believed human beings had to live as minimally as possible and that this sort of lifestyle was not easy for an average human being.

The Stoics' main objective was the endorsement of two-sided approaches and to create a meeting point between those extremes. They believed virtue could be classified as the singularly genuine good attribute adequate to achieve eudemonia without any reference to the circumstances in which an individual found him/herself. Other good things, such as wealth, health, and education, could be plausibly chosen and not just seen in cases such as poverty, sickness, and ignorance. These things are not mixed with others that have natural values.

GREEK STOICISM

The "Greek" era of Stoicism occurred during the first and second ancient stages of the philosophy. It was popular from the time when Zeno created his school until the period during which the branch of knowledge experienced a shift to Rome. That period existed during the reign of Posidonius (100 BC). Posidonius was friends with Cicero, who, although not a Stoic, remains a viable source if Stoicism is traced to its very beginnings.

Stoicism did not just emanate from Athens; it grew rapidly and became largely successful. Many of its teachers, were originally from the Eastern part of the Mediterranean communities. Zeno, its founder, was from Citium, which is now known as Cyprus. Chrysippus hailed from a city in what is now southern Turkey. Cleanthes was from Assos, which was located in modern-day western Turkey. The ethnic diversity of Stoicism's early scholars indicates the dynamism of the cultural backgrounds of the individuals of that era, much of which was the result of Alexander's conquests.

In the initial stages, Stoicism was dominantly Socrates' philosophy. Zeno, the creator, started studying with Cynic Crates, which is why Cynicism teachings continued to reflect the teachings of Stoicism. Its grip was seen even in the late works of Epictetus. Among Zeno's teachers was Polemon, the head of the school, and Stilpo, a student of Socrates. The inclusion was necessary because Zeno planned to expand the philosophy, which, on the one hand, was inspired by Socrates and, on the other hand, was a truce between Stilpo's and Polemon's beliefs. The Socrates' side agreed that there could be other forms of goodness (perhaps not as important as virtue), while the latter side assumed that no other form of goodness could be found outside the stipulated divisions of virtue.

That truce was based on the Stoic principle that other forms of goodness are based on Ethics/ Their values are neutral, although they remain ideals that human beings would naturally pursue.

When studying Stoicism as a philosophical subject, Zeno was able to develop three stages. The first stage was Ethics, described as an abridged form of Cynicism. The second stage explored Physics and had its roots in Timaeus by Plato. It discussed a world that provides room for passive as well as active principles including the occurrence of the principle of causation. The third stage treats Logic as it relates to Stoicism and encompassed terms we now refer to as epistemology and formal Logic; these can also be interpreted as principles of knowledge, which, according to Stoics, was purely natural. (A comprehensive analysis of these stages will appear later in this book.)

Many of the Stoics appeared after Zeno asserted some of his ideas leading them to interpret many of his beliefs in a different way. An instance of this can be seen in the disagreement between Chrysippus and Cleanthes about the idea of unity among all virtues. Zeno explained that every virtue was a type of wisdom. This prompted Cleanthes to assume that he meant wisdom was the only true virtue.

Chrysippus was able to interpret such teachings to mean every virtue has an element of wisdom or is partially attached to wisdom.

Ancient Stoic philosophers were known to have been very dogmatic and, on most occasions, were not critical when interpreting the works of Zeno. An instance is Chrysippus' persistent position regarding his claim that the brain is not where intelligence is formed. He argued that the human heart is where intelligence resides before it spreads to other parts. That position was in contrast to the basic biological findings already known during his time. This ultimately resulted in reproaches from concerned external parties as they were scorned for such opinions. However, Stoics who existed after did well to address the subject.

This error in judgment aside, Chrysippus was a very reputable Stoic whose thoughts instigated a positive turnaround for a Stoic Academy that had been dealt a major blow at the time it was controlled by Cleanthes. Chrysippus introduced comprehensive structures that broadened the scope of Stoic teachings. In Logic, he propounded plausible qualitative notions that formed some of the main philosophical tenets of Stoicism that have stood the test of time. His influence was so apparent that Diogenes Laertius had to note that Chrysippus's writings gave Stoicism its viability.

Sixty years after the reign of Diogenes Laertius, the Stoic school had two leaders: Diogenes of Babylon and Zeno of Tarsus. These two leaders had hardly any meaningful impact on the foundation of Stoicism. If they had contributed in any way, none of it could have overshadowed the achievements and works of Chrysippus. Nothing notable occurred until the year 155 BC when three leaders from the city's three prominent schools (Stoic, Peripatetic, and Academic) were asked to spread their teachings to Rome to foster diplomacy between the two cities.

Note: The Epicurean school was also a prominent school during this period, but its leaders constantly insisted that the school could not be involved in any political matter or contract. Hence, no leader represented the school in Rome.

Those who advanced to Rome – for instance, Diogenes of Babylon, the Stoic leader – impressed the commoners in Rome by their outstanding performances in public spaces. However, these acts were relatively burdensome for the elites who were fast being relegated to the shadows of the city. Ultimately, the acts initiated a long-lasting rivalry between top politicians and the philosophers in Rome, particularly during the era following the Republican Empire. However, the struggle gave rise and prominence of the study of philosophy in Rome leading the city and some study centers to surpass Athens in the field.

Thereafter, the Stoics' partnership with the Academy was readdressed by Panaetius, Posidonius, and Antipater of Tarsus, with a focus on the aforementioned relevance of Timaeus in the theories of Stoicism. Posidonius was drawn to the fact that a Pythagorean was the main character in Plato's Dialogue. Pythagorean was a school of thought that Posidonius had found a way to blend into his teachings as a Stoic.

Obviously, Posidonius and Panaetius had a long-term plan to derive a mutual understanding among Stoicism, Academism, and Aristotelianism, which they had termed as the three aspects of the philosophy of Socrates. This noble plan contributed to the progressive achievements of Stoicism when the leaders of the prominent philosophical schools had to migrate to Rome from Athens.

ROMAN STOICISM

The migration of prominent leaders of the popular philosophical institutes from Athens to Rome attracted keen interest from many Romans. The catalysts of such movements were actually the political practices of the period between 88 BC and 86 BC. Philosophy in the western part of the world took renewed, long-lasting forms, many of which centered around Stoicism.

During those periods, unexpected philosophers such as Epicurean Aristion, as well as Athenion, a Peripatetic, had become political leaders in Athens. They foolishly aligned with Mithridates to wage war against the Romans. Rome subsequently defeated the Athenian leader as well as the King of Pontus. This led to chaos and panic in Athens causing many philosophers to depart to different parts of the Mediterranean.

The last Stoic teacher in Athens, who at the time distanced himself from Rome, was Panaetius. There is no recorded document about the continued existence of the Stoic School (Stoa) after his reign. Posidonius did not teach in Rome; his teachings occurred primarily in Rhodes. The spread and complete shift of Stoic teachings were so definitive that Stoic Augustus appointed Rhodes as an equally serene home for Epicurean studies instead of Tarsus. The almighty Rome became the new settlement for Stoicism.

More importantly, the study of Stoicism rose to the fore in Rome when its governance was about to transition from the Republican system to a city that would rule an empire. Those years were a perilous time. Cato the Younger was an important figure for newer Stoics due to his constant

Philosophy of the ruled

disapproval of the practices of Julius Caesar, whom he labeled a tyrant.

In the late stages of 100 BC, Arius Didymus and Athenodorus of Tarsus were two staunch Stoics who were succeeded by Seneca, a Stoic crusader whose contributions to the advancement of Stoicism were as resounding as they were controversial. The two Stoics provided private counsel to Rome's first emperor, Augustus. In his time, Arius took it upon himself to write a letter to Livia, Augustus' wife, to console her after her son by Augustus met an untimely death. Seneca lauded the letter as a masterpiece of therapy in terms of emotions, and it formed the foundation of many of his works.

In the imperial era, Stoicism made a comprehensive shift from being written as mere theories – its Logic and Physics aspects – to an exemplary and productive philosophy on which the Ethics aspect thrived. The shift never undermined the importance and relevance of Stoicism as a whole. Stoics of that era created a variety of pieces, such as Natural Questions by Seneca, which examined Physics as it relates to his philosophy; Element of Ethics by Hierocles; and Cornutus' Compendium of Greek Theology, a treatise that comprehensively covered Stoic subjects and has proven to be relevant at any stage or age of Stoicism studies.

Prominent Stoics of the period, such as Epictetus and Musonius, were astute teachers. As well, Marcus Aurelius and Seneca were actively involved in politics at the time. Their emancipations, activities, and practices slightly contradicted the roles played by Chrysippus and Zeno whose foundational approaches were largely theoretical.

The late Republican era also witnessed the emergence of

viable but indirect information banks on Stoicism. One instance of this is Cicero's writings, such as Cato Maior de Senectute, De Officiis, Paradox Stoicorum, and many others. Lives of the Eminent Philosophers, written by Diogenes Laertius, was one of the most resourceful books of the period. Even after the infamous regression of Stoicism, the books still inspired other writers. Simplicius, the Neoplatonist, and Plotinus are good examples.

The dominance of Stoicism during the Imperial Era in Rome cannot be overestimated. In fact, its reign extended well beyond a few centuries. Its dominance laid the foundations for Neostoicism during the Renaissance period and still has its grip on the 21st Century's "Modern Stoicism."

The reasons for this resounding dominance can be traced to two distinct acts. The first was the very influential and practical teachings of Epictetus and Musonius. The other was the active political involvement of Marcus and Seneca. Musonius found a way to combine the two acts. Among many other things, he participated in classes for knights in Rome and actively taught Stoicism. His participation in politics was not only constant, but he persistently criticized the policies of Vespasian and Nero, which earned him two separate exiles. In general, Stoics were not very lucky with the emperors whose views and dictates they criticized or opposed. On most occasions, they were brutally persecuted, sent into exile, and even killed. The bulk of these unfortunate events occurred during the regimes of Domitian, Vespasian, and Nero. Nero was known to have ordered Seneca to take his own life, and Domitian was responsible for Epictetus' exile to Greece.

The diverse ways of being a Stoic is another aspect that dominated Roman Stoicism. Musonius could be described as simultaneously resourceful and restrictive. In his writing and speeches, he emphasized the necessity of family and marriage, as well as sacrifices. He opined that philosophical practices were as applicable to women as they were to men. He stressed that women should practice virtue the way men did. Of course, that was contradictory to his beliefs of family and marriage. He also maintained that affairs outside marriage should be justified without any gender bias. On the other hand, Epictetus led a complete quasi-ascetic life. This is vividly exemplified in his discourse, On Cynicism.

Seneca advocated for "preferred indifferents," a position particularly influenced by his senatorial post in Rome. However, this does not render his approach to Stoicism invalid as he clearly noted that he was personally critical of many of the approaches of antecedents. He also declared that he would not turn down the chance to gain knowledge from other schools, such as the Epicurean school. As well, there was Marcus Aurelius' way of being a Stoic. Although his approach was open in nature, he was widely popular for his agnostic views on theology.

These aforementioned distinct practices go a long way toward proving that Stoicism thrived in Rome. It is evident that many of the foundational theories established by the earliest Stoics underwent understandable refinements, many of which were put into practice and good use personally as well as socially.

Note: More on the individual Stoic practices and distinct thoughts of the aforementioned philosophers will be discussed in subsequent chapters.

COMPARISONS TO SOME HELLENISTIC SCHOOLS

The emergence and advancements of different philosophical schools during the Hellenistic era did not occur in isolation.

That is, they were not completely independent of one another. The schools were built by constant interactions with each other. Through the interactions, each was able to either reduce or add to whatever its scholars had learned from the dominant practices of other schools. Most importantly, there is the adoption and blend of Cynicism from the early beginnings of Stoicism to Epictetus' judicious use of the notion. There were agreements and disagreements that Stoicism and its scholars had with Aristotelianism, Platonism, and Epicureanism scholars.

Epictetus was very direct and concise in his perceptions of Epicureans. He had opposing beliefs which he constantly emphasized. He highlighted the differences between Epicureans' ideas about pleasure and pain and the strict attention Stoics paid to integrity and the virtue of human beings' characters.

In his Discourses, Epictetus mentioned that, according to the Epicureans, tranquility of the mind – more precisely, ataraxia – is the product of creating pleasure and removing any form of pain. Stoics, however, have a similar name and explanation for such conditions. Apatheia – or better still, the absence of disturbing emotions – is commonly used by Stoics.

A section of Epictetus' discourse titled 'Against the Epicureans and the Academics' also showcases his absolute distaste for many theories from other schools, which he labeled unrealistic and lacking in common sense. Furthermore, he explained that Epicurus was a confused individual who preached refraining from the complexities of society and leading a lowly life, yet took the time to write a book about it. According to Epictetus, this shows that Epicurus was concerned about the lifestyles of others in society. He explained that Epicurus' human nature, which is not only common to everyone but also the strongest part of one's being, pushed him to go against his supposed practices.

In his Discourses, Epictetus also criticized some skeptics within the Academics. He asked rhetorical questions about what they actually thought they were doing. He stressed that they contradicted their proofs every day, yet refused to stop making futile efforts. He asked where they would shove their food when they ate and stated it would be either their eyes or mouths. He also asked where they went to take their baths and whether they had ever switched the roles of their dishes, i.e., using a saucepan or a skewer as a spoon. All his questions seem justifiable, not on Stoicism's theories but on its practical approaches. He stressed that if rational explanations could be given about those involved in adultery, politicians who mismanage funds meant for the public, or a young man engaging in rebellious acts against his parents, would there be any difference between what is good and what is not? Are there acts that are vicious and acts that could be seen as virtuous?

Despite Epictetus' criticisms, some early Stoics did not completely snub the Epicurean and Academic approaches. Marcus Aurelius' agnostic nature on atoms and providence, and Seneca's sympathy for many Epicurean approaches, prove this. Seneca's Stoicism practices highlight that he was able to blend ideas from other schools with ideas of the Stoics. In his piece Natural Questions, he stated that he never agreed completely with the ideas from the Stoic school.

In De Finibus, Cicero was able to highlight some instances of disagreement between Aristotelians and Stoics through an imagined interaction involving Cato the Younger. Cicero explained that Carneades did not stop his arguments based on the fact that the famous issue of "good and evil" had little or no difference in its interpretation by the Peripatetics and the Stoics. He emphasized that the only noticeable difference was the terms used in their descriptions. He mentioned that verbal differences mean little when the practical aspects of the schools' assertions are similar. He stated that the Peripatetics believed everything they stood for could be categorized as the good things that lead to happiness. The Stoic school was of the opinion that whatever constituted absolute happiness had a certain level of value within it. This explanation was intended to address the different approaches to what Stoics and Aristotelians categorized as "external goods."

An array of comprehensive documents indicates how some Stoic ideas were reformed in response to the challenges and criticisms from rival schools. An example is the Stoics' refined stance about Determinism as it had been used by Philopator. This was a productive outcome of the scrutiny from the Middle-Age Platonist and the Peripatetic philosophers. There are also multiple examples of the incorporation of Stoic approaches into the teachings of other schools, as seen in Antiochus of Ascalon's situation. He inculcated Stoic principles when he tried to reconstruct Platonism. He also emphasized that Aristotle and Zeno created some notions which Plato had suggested.

Another instance, which will be discussed in detail later, is how Stoicism was able to blend into Christianity during the Middle Age of Platonism, a time between 150 CE and 215 CE, which was also the era of Alexandria.

CHAPTER 2: THE FIRST TWO TOPOI

Ethics is fundamental to Stoics teachings and critical insight into Ethics necessitates the need for the support of two distinct areas of inquisitions: Physics and Logic. With these other fields came the term "The Three Topoi of Stoicism." An in-depth explanation of this trio will be given, but it is crucial to examine how they are related to one another.

Stoicism is not just a philosophy of theories; it was created primarily with the noble desire to help individuals achieve a eudemonic lifestyle. According to Stoics, this could be attained as long as individuals constantly upheld some forms of virtue. During Stoic's popularity in Rome, the focus moved away from its original notion to the idea of "apatheia." This shift was successful due to the Ethics "topos" of Stoicism. The change in focus was assisted by Stoics' mastery of the remaining two topoi. Logic was, at the time, a more elaborate subject than its modern-day meanings and applications imply as it included Logic "sensu stricto." Logic was also an embodiment of cognitive science as well as theories of knowledge (epistemology).

Physics was famously interpreted by the Stoics as what is categorized in the modern world as metaphysics, theology, and natural science. Early Stoics perceived Physics as the study of their society while Logic was a branch of knowledge that enlightened people on how to create a perception of their entire world.

Physics and Logic are similar to Ethics because Stoicism is a type of philosophy that is entirely naturalistic. When Stoics mention "souls" or "God," they often refer to real human beings to blend in with the natural beliefs of human beings and to ensure their teachings remain as rational as possible to individuals. Stoics were fond of creating imagery to explain the connections between Ethics, Logic, and Physics. Proof of this can be traced to a Stoicism piece: Diogenes Laertius. A very popular instance of imagery is the Stoic Egg. The red portion was equated to Physics, the white portion was seen as Ethics, and the shell was assumed to be Logic. The comparison is somewhat confusing when the original biological examination of eggs is considered. Ethics should actually be nurtured by Physics and, hence, the Physics portion should have been the white part, while the Ethics portion should have been the red part.

In a more plausible way, one can liken the relationship between the three topoi to the components of a garden. The fence would be charged with protecting the plants within the garden and creating the boundary can be equated to Logic. The fertile soil of the garden provides essentials nutrients for the plants and can be said to be Physics because it was seen as the true knowledge of the world. Finally, the proceeds of the plants can be regarded as Ethics as it remained the main focus of Stoicism discourses.

Stoics had disagreements about certain issues, such as the exact pattern in which all the topoi had to be analyzed and taught to their students. Their opinions differed from one another in terms of the benefits of some curricula as is seen in the modern world's teaching practices. However, unlike what dominates morals-centered philosophy in the Modern Age, ancient Stoics practiced a naturalistic philosophy in which no clear difference exists between "what it is" and "what it ought to be." This is because they believed what an individual should do largely depends on the individual's knowledge of the way the world works and, more importantly, the individual's ability to think rationally. The next sections examine Logic,

Physics, and Ethics as they relate to Stoicism.

LOGIC

Ancient Stoics contributed immensely to early discoveries of Logic and to epistemology as is proven by the huge collection of books on this subject. Stoics maintained that "The Sage," a representation of a perfect human, could master the inherent knowledge of all things. In practical aspects, they largely depended on the gradual progression of morals and cognition because Physics and Logic share basic similarities and partially function like the third topos, Ethics. The idea was eventually named "prokope," which translates simply as "making progress." Stoics constantly repelled the criticisms from Academic Skeptics who believed the notion could not be justifiably defended.

In contrast to the strict stance of the Epicureans of their notions, Stoics ensured they were not dogmatic concerning their notions and the general impressions they tried to convey. Rather, they labeled some of them "cataleptic." This infers that they led to good levels of understanding while they also acknowledged that others could not have followed the same path. In his explanation, Diogenes Laertius stated that Stoics' cataleptic notions stemmed from existing or realistic things and are equally in tune with those from which they stem. Cataleptic notions have their imprints on the things from which they have been drawn and verified. Diogenes also explained that notions that are not cataleptic must be from things not in existence; even if they are from existing things, the notions will not conform to their origins if assessed appropriately. Hence, they lack clarity and are not particularly distinct.

Stoics acknowledged that people's beliefs might not always be correct, such as when one has dreamed, hallucinated, or even created some form of conclusions in the mind through an unconscious process of judging things or people. However, Stoics emphasized that continuous and comprehensive tutoring would help one improve at marking the difference between notions that are cataleptic or otherwise. This would ultimately enable such individuals to determine whether to give their consent.

Chrysippus further opined that it is necessary to entertain multiple notions because through these absorption processes, concepts form. In the long run, progress occurs. According to the Stoics, knowledge is empirical in composition. This notion was reinforced when Skeptical critiques eventually settled for it and labeled their explanations as what is now referred to as the "most suitable explanation."

Furthermore, a notion that is cataleptic cannot be said to be knowledge itself. In essence, Stoics tried to create a clear difference between a trio of opinion, apprehension, and knowledge in general. They expressed the notion that agreeing with cataleptic notions is merely a stage in the process of achieving genuine knowledge. Knowledge, on its own, has stability and comprehensive structures, which is more than what any notion or impression could offer. The Stoics' idea of justification is largely coherent; this can also be seen in their stance on the theory of truth.

R.J Hankinson gave his opinion of an intriguing part of the disagreement that occurred between Academic Skeptics and the Stoics; this was about the epistemic assent to be given to Stoics' cataleptic notions. He tried to highlight and question the reasons why the notions are termed distinct and clear. Hankinson explained that if distinctiveness and clarity are integral parts of cataleptic notions, they are also impeccable aspects of the notions. However, contradictory situations could be drawn. Hankinson noted that one member of a pair of twins could be addressed as the other due to their similar identities.

This example is one of the situations that informed the advancement of Stoics' pattern of thinking when responding to pressures from external sources. According to Cicero, Zeno knew that a valid notion might have originated from an existing or non-existing thing. Therefore, he re-arranged his position on the issue through the addition of a clause interpreted as having been an improvement on the Stoics' belief that no two things can be a perfect clone of each other, even though the pair could appear as such on some occasions.

Frede also corroborated the assertion by explaining that the clarity and distinctiveness of cataleptic notions are not based on the intrinsic composition of the notions. Instead, they are based on the same external factors or aspects which can be traced to their origins. Hence, epistemology in Stoicism is not internally determined, but externally determined. Goldman (1980) stated that, due to Skeptics' consistent criticisms, Stoics had become those on whom to rely when it came to issues of knowledge.

Furthermore, Athenaeus once described a tale that involved Sphaerus, who was Chrysippus' colleague and Cleathes' student at the time. During a banquet, Sphaerus's attention was called to some birds. As soon as he made a move to grab one of the birds, he realized they were merely carved from wax. The gesture prompted accusations against him because he was seen as having believed an illusory concept. Although, in a clever way, he indicated that he had given such acknowledgment because it wasn't beyond valid reasoning to have assumed that the birds were real. He believed he could only have been rightly criticized if he had insisted the wax figures were, in fact, real birds.

The aforementioned explanations depict some peripheral assessment of Logic as it relates to Stoicism. This school of philosophy contributed greatly to the modern-day's rather shallow description and examination of it. Ancient Stoics' pattern of thinking portrays the fact that not all viable positions on an issue can be said to possess syllogism. This is in contrast to the Aristotelian way of thinking, which has a more relevant influence on Logic in the modern world.

For more clarity, five different forms of syllogisms constitute Stoics' assessment of Logic. They have been fortified with four other argumentative guidelines which could ultimately be employed to incorporate any other form of syllogism into part of the five highlighted ones. A much wider treatment of Logic by Stoics shows that the field was assumed to be propositional in nature, as is seen in parts of the writings of Frege.

Logic in Stoicism showcases the dichotomies between what is known as assertibles and sayables. The sayables category, which is the wider of the two, consists of oaths, invocations, imperatives, curses, and questions, as well as assertibles. On the other hand, assertibles can be referred to as self-completing sayables which are used in making certain declarations or statements.

A practical explanation follows. "If Chrysippus is in Greece, then Chrysippus is in Rome" is an assertion which is conditional in composition. The statement can be said to have been coined from two distinct assertions, which are "Chrysippus is in Greece" and "Chrysippus is in Rome." Therefore, the prominent distinction between the propositions of Frege and the assertibles of Stoics is that time is an important factor in determining the truthfulness or falsehood of some assertions. That is, "Chrysippus is in Greece" might not be true today, but could become the truth tomorrow. The assertion could become false a month later. Importantly, an assertible is not without falsehood or truthful aspect. In fact, the truthfulness or untruthfulness of a statement is an important criterion for it to be considered an assertible. This means it is impossible to make assertions or declarative statements about things whose properties cannot be verified as true or false.

Stoics focused on how valid any argument was. They were not necessarily concerned about concise truths or reasonable statements. This is relative to Stoics' interest in using Logic as a form of protection for their central subject matter, Ethics. Stoics also inculcated adjustments and classifications in their customary discussion of Logic. They structured plausibility, necessity, possibility, impossibility, probability, and non-possibility. The approach was interestingly practical and appeared to be modern in form. It was used to highlight the point that an assertible may be unavoidably believed even when it has been discovered to be untrue. Stoics were able to call people's attention to the fact that some assertibles are naturally not likely to be false.

In conclusion, Stoics, particularly Chrysippus, sensed things easily, which prompted them always to make provisions for paradoxes that are somewhat logical. The liar and sorites paradoxes, for example, have been said to have a relation to "vagueness" in semantics.

PHYSICS

The topos of Physics, according to the Stoics, is what has come to be known as metaphysics, theology, and natural science in the modern world. The following explains these divisions.

In the aspect of cosmology and natural science, Stoics are known to be very sentimental about living while paying close attention to the dictates of nature. This leads to a persistent striving to understand nature itself. This also highlights the differences between ancient and recent views of natural science. The study of natural science can be said to be a means or a path toward one's pursuit of a eudemonic life. Stoics hold the opinion that all things that have been conventionally agreed to exist have a physical form. They believed the human soul, and even God, have a physical representation. They identified some things as being incorporeal; these include time, sayables, and the void. In a way, these latter categories appear to be a contrast to Stoicism's strong stance on materialism. However, they aren't very distinct when compared to a modern naturalist view, which also offers access to anyone who can constructively discuss some abstract subjects. Originally, such aspects were the core of materialism as only physical beings are capable of having such thoughts.

Stoics dominantly practiced what can be referred to as a "vitalist" approach to the appraisal of nature, which can be divided into two basic parts. The first is an active principle which relates to God and reasoning, while the second is a passive principle which discusses matter and substance. Furthermore, the active principle is not destructible and cannot be generated or regenerated. The passive principle, which shares similarities with water, air, earth, and fire (also known as the four elements) can be recreated after a cosmic destruction, which is an important aspect of cosmology in Stoicism.

Moreover, Stoics contradicted the Aristotelians' idea concerning the existence and idea of a "central mover." They also completely ignored God according to the definition made by Christians. (Christians describe God as being unlimited in terms of time and space.) Stoics' stand on this aspect also boils down to the fact that they believed things that cannot be seen in the physical realm do not have the power to put things in place as no rational relationship or connection exists between them. This stance led to the emergence of a biologically interpreted process of the law of cause and effect – an interpretation that completely contrasts with post-Cartesian and Newton's mechanics-based philosophy.

According to Stoics, universal conflagrations repeatedly occur in the same form because nature or God has organized some occurrences in the most suitable way to be done from the onset. Hence, no plausible cause exists to change things again. To an extent, this claim is correct, particularly because every law of cause and effect appears to be predetermined and somewhat fixed. It would be intriguing to carefully examine recent cosmology-based notions that have predicted that occurrences and the general progression of things in the universe keep repeating themselves, although none seem to recognize a divine or supernatural being.

Eusebius once opined that, in the case of universal conflagration, the originating fire could be compared to a seed with a complete set of principles on all things, as well as the knowledge of what triggered all the things that have happened, are currently happening, and those that will happen later. He mentioned that these occurrences have a form and order which are equally a function of knowledge, fate, and truth. They are an unavoidable set of rules that guide existing things in general.

In his book De Fato, Cicero outlined the concept of causation according to Stoicism. He drew a conclusion on the similarity of fate and its initial cause. Meanwhile, Chrysippus clearly emphasized that for every motion or occurrence, a corresponding cause exists. This implies that absolutely nothing exists without cause or reason. The notion of worldwide causality prompted Stoics to adopt Divination as an aspect of Physics and not just another superstitious notion. This is documented in Cicero's De Divinatione, and it is sensible to a large extent, once the Stoics' idea of an opinion of the cosmos has been adequately comprehended.

Stoics' principal notion about this is that making suggestions or predictions about things that have yet to happen is not a practice carried out without the inclusion of the known laws of Physics. Hence, such predictions can be made only through the judicious exploitation of those laws.

Ancient Stoics could be said to be determinists. Cicero had stated that a particular act should not have a particular outcome on one occasion and change in another. Rather, such acts should have a constant, similar outcome at all times. Stoics never believed in chance, although they had some conceptions about it. They felt that human beings only ignorantly believe in it. Stoics emphasized that humans see some occurrences as random only because such occurrences are not adequately comprehended.

The implication of Physics as it relates to Stoics' central topos is that Ethics is apparent. Cicero justifiably and concisely explained that Chrysippus had the idea of creating a balance between a constricted incompatibility theory and a libertarian theory. In 2003, White offered some explanations: just as it was found in the works of Spinoza, he mentioned that although the focus was initially on moral responsibility, it was subsequently placed on dignity as well as the worth of morals.

Regarding ontology, Stoics never shared similarities or mutual opinions with the Epicureans or the Atomists, and they were strictly against Corpuscularianism. This stems from the fact that they believed the notion of atoms is a direct violation of their idea of a smooth connection, interaction, and flow among the things that occur in the universe. Interestingly, the Stoics' idea of this sort of conformity is somewhat related to many modern theories of mechanics in which our world is composed of a singular wave function. However, such comparison or interpretation has outlived its relevance and is no longer applicable.

ETHICS

Even if other aspects of Stoicism's propositions are categorized as mere theories, Ethics is far beyond that. Much of the opinions and assertions about it are largely practical. Ethics was described as the study of laid-down prescriptions on the way human beings should live their lives in general. The middle-age Stoicism proponents had the submission that Ethics was central to philosophy as a whole. Admittedly, its mastery is anything but easy. In Discourses, Epictetus emphasized that a room where philosophy is to be taught can be likened to a hospital: a place one is not expected to exit with much comfort, as one was not originally in good shape upon arrival. Epictetus chose to view control as seen in the way it was explained in the Manual of Epictetus: There are things for which we can be held directly responsible, but there are other things for which human beings, in general, are not accountable. This means human beings can control some situations, while they cannot control others.

In a way, the appraisal of Ethics by ancient Stoics was not very practical in nature. Stoics such as Zeno, Chrysippus, and Cleanthes primarily tried to create a system for their ideologies. They were consistently fighting against the criticisms from Academic Skeptics and the Epicureans concerning their theories. "Follow Nature" was the Stoicism school's popular phrase for Ethics. This can be interpreted as "let nature guide you on the way to live." The idea of this phrase acknowledges the realistic-providential part of the sequentially designed universe (the cosmos) and the normal identifiable nature of human beings - one the Stoics perceive to be a social being with the ability to develop reasonable submissions pertaining to the difficulties in his or her life. A narrow examination of Zeno's original description of the Ethics principle is "live consistently." Cleanthes is the other early Stoic who sought to make the phrase clearer and more understandable with the addition of "with nature." This notion can be closely linked to oikeiôsis, which, most often, is interpreted as meaning appropriation.

Stoics believe that humans, by default, possess the innate ability to nurture their morals. This ability starts with what is now widely known as an instinct which is modified as a child approaches the stage of reasoning. An important fact to note is that Stoics' naturalistic view of the origin and classification of good morals has a very similar inclination toward recent studies and research in cognitive and evolutionary sciences.

From the onset, human beings act in such a way as to promote and achieve their desires, aims, and what interests them or keeps them in good shape. Human beings try to relate to the things that interest their parents and, by extension, members of their immediate community. Another natural instinct or pattern of behavior exhibited by human beings is trying to grasp things in which to engage so as to tackle events that happen throughout life. The Stoics equated these natural tendencies to four main virtues: courage, practical wisdom, justice, and temperance. Courage and temperance are seen as virtues necessary to strive toward any human goal or desire. Justice is described as human beings' innate worries about a continuously growing population of human beings in their communities and the universe at large. Practical wisdom describes human beings' abilities and techniques that are used to tackle positive and negative events that occur in life.

This explanation underlines the relationship between all the virtues as highlighted by the Stoics. A good place to start to understand their ideas on this aspect of their philosophy is to identify and examine other subordinating virtues which fall under the four virtues.

Practical wisdom has other components, such as discretion, good judgment, and resourcefulness. Courage also has divisions, such as confidence, magnanimity, and perseverance. The third virtue, temperance has components, such as self-control, propriety, and sense of honor. The virtue of justice was broadened to encompass sociability, piety, and kindness. However, virtue was dominantly addressed as a unitary subject encompassing the components and classifications. Moreover, the four main classifications have Socrates' and Plato's origin, which makes it possible to unify all the virtues as highlighted by the Stoics.

For instance, courage can be seen as having the wisdom to inculcate endurance. Justice can be equated to the application of practical wisdom in living socially. Temperance can also represent wisdom especially when it comes to making choices. Chrysippus critically examined the pluralistic concept embedded in the overall unity of the virtues. He concluded that the classifications cannot be separated, as Stoics believe no one can claim to possess an adequate virtue of courage and still be temperamental.

Pierre Hadot, a philosopher of French descent, once compared the three topoi, the four outlined virtues, and the disciplines of desire, action, and assent. Desire as a Stoic principle is occasionally labeled as acceptance in Stoicism. It emanated from its Physics field of study – precisely, from the notion of causation. Desire explores the process of personal training in a bid to be interested in the general things expected by one's world, and not otherwise.

A metaphorical analysis that had been used by Epictetus to explain this is a situation in which a dog is kept in a cart. The dog has the option to wrestle against the progression of the cart at all turns. This would ultimately cause the dog to harm itself, become sad or dejected in the process. On the other hand, the dog can decide to move according to the dictates of the cart earning itself a good cruise. By extension, this analysis translates into Nietzsche's definition of "amor fati," which means "love your fate." It also formed the basis of Epictetus' expression "endure and renounce," which means one is expected to endure the things that come one's way in life and avoid the things the world does not give room for or permit. Hadot opined that Desire as a principle is very much interwoven with or related to the temperance and courage virtues.

Action, another discipline, is otherwise known as Philanthropy. It is principal to the identified virtues. Its main concern is the fact that humans must grow and inculcate innate forms of concern or responsibility for one another in ways that are in line with the practice of justice as a virtue. This discipline has most of its rudiments in the teachings of Ethics. A suitable expression that clearly depicts its description can be extracted from Meditations by Aurelius. It explains that human beings live for the advantage of others like them. They enlighten themselves and also learn to cope with one another. Aurelius' proposition is a vivid representation of Stoic philanthropy. The idea of coping highlights the emperor's conception that human-being-to-human-being enlightenment is a responsibility that should be carried out by indulging others in positive things or going through difficulties together.

The third discipline, Assent, is commonly labeled "mindfulness." It is important to note that even though the word is spelled the same, the Stoics' idea of the word is totally different from that of the Buddhists. (More on assent as it relates to emotions and psychology will be discussed later.)

Assent explains the Stoics' idea of the importance of deciding on or arriving at conclusions about those things to inculcate and absorb and those that one should not occur during one's interaction with the universe. This means Assent deals with ways to decide appropriately. It apparently relates to Logic in Stoicism, as well as Practical Wisdom. An expression by Seneca interpreted as preparing or fortifying one's mind to accept and live with one's problems, adequately suits this last discipline.

One can deduce that Ethics, according to the Stoics, is centered on the notion of virtue and its unitary and diverse dispensations by the Stoics. This is similar to the notions of the Cynics who, in contrast to the Peripatetics, did not provide room for a long list of things, such as health, education, or even wealth, to be the prerequisites for living a life that is eudemonic. Peripatetics cannot agree with the Stoics' notion of a eudemonic Sage.

Ethics, according to the Stoics, seeks to achieve an agreement between the stylishly elitist notions upheld by the Peripatetics, and the rather ascetic notions of the Cynics. This is carried out by introducing the somewhat controversial idea of indifferents, which are either preferred or not. Zeno's now-missing book on Ethics is known to have encompassed the nitty-gritty of the concept. Some of Diogenes' writings explain that Zeno created a form of distinction – valuable indifferents and those that don't have value. Those with value are called "axia," and the others are called "apaxia." In axia, wealth, education, and good health exist. Apaxia consists of things such as ignorance, poverty, and sickness. The creation of the indifferents has its importance as it helps Stoics draw inferences from the Peripatetic and the Cynic schools. There are indifferents that are generally chosen above others provided that these indifferents do not obstruct the practice of virtue. However, there are some reasons for labeling them as indifferents; they are not necessarily important in trying to live a eudemonic life. This means although an innate desire exists in every human being to strive for the preferred indifferents, human beings have the ability to lead a life of integrity and ultimately achieve eudemonia in the process even though they experience negative circumstances.

Ethics in Stoicism extends beyond what has been discussed so far. More structures will be examined subsequently. It is important to stress the relationship between the notion of Ethics in Stoicism and the providence notions about the universe which are adopted in its Physics field of study. Stoics have established that studying Physics boosts one's understanding of Ethics. They proclaimed that the structure of the cosmos is somewhat providential. However, the aforementioned view cannot be said to be the only process of achieving a eudemonic life.

Gregory Vlastos stated that the theocratic notion is not a hindrance to the idea of the perceived relationship between the cosmos and virtue. Leading a virtuous life is, in fact, a form of alignment with the supposed order. Vlastos emphasized that such alignment does not mean the requirements of virtue would change; the concept of eudemonia remains unchanged. Things retain their standards because Physics influences Ethics in ways that are not predetermined. This also means that although Ethics depends largely on Physics, Physics cannot be used as its focal point. Ethics in Stoicism has a rather modern dispensation due to its naturalistic notions.

Vlastos' emphasis can be reinforced by many Stoicism-related sources, especially in the works of Marcus Aurelius. Some writings on Stoicism do not specifically examine the interaction between Physics and Ethics. Epictetus opined that the substances (fire, earth, and atoms) that form the universe do not matter much to him. He stated that it was ideal to be aware of only the disposition of what is good and what is not, the heights of human desires, as well as their limits, and instincts to either act on or suppress. Epictetus was convinced that these highlighted processes or guidelines are just enough to live an ideal life enabling humans to ignore things that are not within their reach. He stressed that elusive, unreachable, or incomprehensible things, by default, have been set to be that way for human beings. Even if by chance one obtains knowledge of such things, there is arguably no gain in doing so. Epictetus mentioned that those who necessitate such discoveries for their philosophical submissions do so in vain. He emphasized that the structure of nature (Stoics' supposed controller of the universe), the ways in which it directs the activities of the universe, and the truth of its existence are mysterious inquisitions about which human beings do not necessarily have to worry.

Epictetus' expression on the matter led Ferraiolo to the conclusion that practices that are metaphysical in nature,

God's existence, and a universe that is rationally controlled, are not entirely fused into the practical aspects of Stoicism or the philosophy's tenets for a eudemonic life.

The foundational concepts that led to the emergence of Stoicism might have been deduced from some presupposed notions that the universe has a divinely constructed order. The effectiveness of Stoic teachings and practices does not directly thrive on universal design, creations, or other sorts of cosmological rules. Generally one can accept the fact that early Stoics widely believed in the existence of a physical ruler of the universe whom they thought responsible for the organization of activities or occurrences within it. They also had the notion that this physical control is pantheist in structure.

Ancient Stoics opined that having a grasp of the cosmos leads to the adequate grasp of Ethics, which they term as the correct field of inquiry on the way to live. One can state or argue that the disposition of metaphysics in Stoicism created a lack of certainty or viability in their teachings on Ethics. The reason is that they created a space for atoms or a God figure. This means Stoics, in a way, conceded to the Epicureans' criticisms.

THE RELATIONSHIP OF APATHEIA AND THE TREATMENT OF EMOTIONS IN STOICISM

Brennan stated that the Stoics' naturalistic approach to Ethics created a fusion between "what is" and "what ought to be" through a comprehensive interpretation of moral developments that occur in humans. The subsequent paragraphs will examine the main contrast between the Epicureans and the Stoics paying close attention to two principal terminologies that the two schools have used to explain the state of mind they consider desirable. Later, attention will be shifted to the classification of emotions in

Stoicism.

Epictetus had been able to create a dichotomy of the Epicurean school, the Garden, and the Stoic school: the Stoa. In a letter, Seneca, who popularly states his tactics of prying into the works of other schools, once informed his friend Lucilius that on some occasions he would gladly make use of some of Epicurus' notions whenever and wherever he felt they were sensible.

In the introductory notes is an explanation of the Stoic belief that the most important aspect of anyone's life is the acquisition and cultivation of virtue. Epicureans felt that the importance of human existence is to do away with anything related to pain, but find ways to experience pleasure.

Both schools have the same notion of what is necessary to achieve eudemonia. While Epicureans referred to the notion as ataraxia, Stoics termed it apatheia. However, noticeable contrasts still exist between the two notions, specifically in the aspects of what the schools believed, how they instructed their students, the ways to carry out such needed activities, and the states of mind cultivated by their students.

An IEP article explains apatheia as a component of eudemonia, which means liberty from passion. Ataraxia is also described as a state of being imperturbable and trouble free, and having a tranquil existence that leads to a eudemonic life. This description reveals that the two terms are constituents of eudemonia. Even though ataraxia is common to the Epicureans, Stoics also used it in different instances.

An important thing to note is that the Stoics' use of "passion" is different from the modern use of the word. In fact, it has little or no relation to "emotion" as it widely is represented in the modern world.

One cannot precisely state that the Stoics preached against passion or life in which humans must suppress their feelings or emotions. The Stoics created a distinction between passions that are healthy and those that are not. Those classified as healthy are a delight, willingness, and discretion, while the unhealthy ones are craving, pain, pleasure, and fear. With the exception of pain, which doesn't have a direct contrast, other divisions of unhealthy passions are the opposite of the healthy ones. The Stoics do not construe "passion" as being innate or based on natural instincts that make it impossible to snub its experience. Rather, passion is seen as a product of human judgment, as well as the result of consenting to an opinion.

Fear, according to the Stoics, is not the largely uncontrollable instinctive response human beings have whenever they are confronted with dangerous situations. Instead, Stoics describe fear as revolving around the action that occurs after such responses and one's perceived view of the cause of the spontaneous response. This also means the Stoics are aware that some reactions are spontaneous and largely uncontrollable, which is the reason their focus is on things human beings can control. They focused on judgments about the probable reasons for the unpremeditated responses. Marcus Aurelius termed the part of human beings that prompts such reactions as the Ruling Faculty. In modern scientific concept, the human brain does this.

Neuroscience in the modern world is similar to the Stoics' idea of human emotions. Joseph LeDoux was able the highlight the difference between the psychological and neuroscientific definitions of "emotion." For instance, neuroscientists believe fear is a product of defense as well as a reaction technique that is neither conscious nor voluntary; the amygdala is its main correlate. Psychologists' definition of "fear" is a difficult-to-understand string of emotions built partly as a defense and reaction technique that the human being's mind interprets cognitively. This view has some resemblance to the Stoic explanation of the term. However, the definitions from the two fields of knowledge are not direct contradictions; instead, they complement one another.

The cognitive description of the emotion of fear is generated from the infusion of a human being's environment and upbringing, conscious thoughts, experiences, memories in one's mind, and some others. In Stoicism, the psychological explanation of emotion is regarded as "passions." The research Joseph carried out reinforces the Stoics' description as well as the viability of their concept of assent.

Pain, in Stoic terminology, is not just a sensation. Rather, it is the inability to do without things that human beings incorrectly judge as bad. Fear is seen as the unpleasant expectancy of things that are dangerous or would cause harm. Stoics perceive "craving" as the annoying struggle to achieve things that have been incorrectly assumed as good. They see pleasure as an equally annoying and unnecessary.

Apatheia is perceived as the product of the reasonable avoidance of things considered harmful. It is a reasonable endeavor for virtue, as well as an understandable lust for virtue. The three qualities of apatheia explain the Stoic submission on discretion, willingness, and delight. The aforementioned explanations validate the reasons for classifying apatheia as a mastery of self-control and calmness when human beings face the things life has in store for them. That is, if human beings use good reasoning, no one would be disturbed by some of the things the Stoics considered as having no relevance, while simultaneously causing everyone to revel in those considered relevant.

It is also very important to note that the Epicurean and Stoic schools documented different routes to achieve ataraxia and apatheia. According to the Epicureans, Ataraxia is a goal that could be achieved when one tries to avoid pain, which also implies one's complete withdrawal from political and social life. Epicurus opined that it was a good thing to be in the company of close friends, but the decision to fully partake in political ventures will definitely lead such individuals to mental and physical pain; hence, such ventures should be ignored.

Stoics stressed the need to put virtue into practice leading to the acceptance of their roles in the social lives of human beings. For example, Aurelius, in his Meditations, emphasized that Stoics always ensured they woke up to carry out human jobs. The interpretation of this is that society needs their help and, hence, they should be useful. Hierocles clarified the Stoic and Cynic cosmopolitan notion, which in a way shows that the Stoics' view of apatheia wasn't a goal in the strict sense of the word; it was, instead, a positive result of leading a life of virtue.

CHAPTER 3: THE POSITION OF STOICISM AFTER THE HELLENISTIC PERIOD

Professor Long from Berkeley once clarified that although it is not widely recognized, Stoicism was relevant across different fields of western philosophy that arose during the Middle Ages, the Renaissance period, and the Modern Age. In his book A Stoic and Socratic Guide to Life, Long identified a number of staunch and partial Stoic philosophers of those periods, such as Leibniz, Spinoza, Rousseau, Augustine, Descartes, More, Kant, and Smith. David Hume is someone who shouldn't be left out. The Renaissance period witnessed the production of books on Stoicism, examples of which are Seneca's Letter and Enchiridion by Epictetus. Enthusiasts comprehensively studied some books that champion Stoic teachings and ideas; De Officiis by Cicero is an example.

Christian views during those periods aligned more with the Stoics' view than those of the Epicureans. The one-sided alignment stems from the fact that the Epicureans' belief of cosmic conflagration and pleasure contradict Christian theology. Christianity's relationship with Stoicism is quite complex in structure; the Stoic stance on pantheism and materialism was frowned upon and ultimately rejected. Unknown to the Stoics was that the notion of "the Logos" was somewhat absorbed into Christianity. The Stoics' teachings on virtue are equivalent to what Christians believe to be the best provision for their followers as they await the second coming of Jesus Christ.

This similarity brought about the indefinite stance that Christians have when it comes to Stoic practices. Augustine, in the initial stages of his writings, favored Stoicism, although he subsequently criticized some of its notions. Tertullian had a positive notion of Stoic practices, and even monasteries used some editions of the Enchiridion. Stoic Ethics famously influenced the works of John of Salisbury, as well as Peter Abelard. Thomas Aquinas had a critical view of the philosophy in regards to the initial attempts made by David of Dinant in a bid to revive Stoicism early in the 13th Century.

Eventually, Stoicism was revived during the Renaissance period as a result of the effective contributions of Justus Lipsius. Lipsius was a philologist and humanist. He produced useful revisions of Tacitus and Seneca. His most successful work was De Constantia in which he explained that Christianity has a lot to gain from Stoicism, especially when its followers are troubled at certain periods in their lives. He also highlighted some concepts of Stoicism that cannot be applied to Christianity.

Lipsius is another philosopher who drew inferences from Epictetus' Enchiridion, which had just gone through its first-ever English interpretation. Some other non-Hellenistic Stoics are Guillaume Du Vair, a statesman of French descent; Francisco de Quevedo, a Spanish author; Pierre Charron; and Michel de Montaigne, the Stoic who dedicated a complete essay to defending Seneca's teachings.

The Neostoicism period was plagued with ups and downs. Before the emergence of Lipsius, criticisms of the revival of apatheia had already been circulated. Pascal and Calvin were the main proponents of such arguments. To guard against such criticisms, Stellars noted that the Stoic texts in the era always had precautionary statements. The Stoics explained that philosophy has a profitable relationship with Christianity if its teachings are used in the right way. No other form of philosophy is more applicable and similar in terms of what Christianity is built upon than Stoicism.

There were multiple instances of support for the philosophy during the Renaissance period. Some of this support even came from professionals in fields other than philosophy. However, Stoicism during the era did not develop into a movement. The notable contributions of Stoicism can be traced only to Montaigne and the writings of Lipsius.

The most relevant Stoicism-inclined philosopher in the modern era is Spinoza, whom Leibniz alleged must have connived with Descartes and eventually led a group of newly indoctrinated Stoics. Spinoza's notion about the structure of the universe bears many similarities to the Stoics'. The two fields acknowledge the existence of an ever-present and all-knowing entity that is seen as nature and also perceived as being behind the law of cause and effect.

The Stoics' interpretations of the cosmos exist in two phases. That contradicts Spinoza's unilateral interpretation of the same concept, but the active and passive roles of the Stoics are intertwined. This gives the rules a unitary status. The precise distinction between Spinoza's ideas and those of the Stoics is the fact that Spinoza perceived God as having qualities that are inestimable, extensive, and infinite. This is in direct contrast to the Stoics' notion of a finite God or nature. Stoicism is monistic in that it treats God as being behind all things that occur. It becomes dualistic as a result of its divisions of extension and thoughts. Stoicism can also be viewed as hierarchical in terms of the way it describes the different categories of God's qualities in some human beings. Furthermore, it is a practicable, realistic, and determinist type of philosophy. Spinoza also mentioned that his idea of Ethics and that of the Stoics share striking similarities making his Ethics an offshoot of Stoic Ethics.

In addition to the differences between the two fields, Spinoza never consented to the existence of teleology about the universe. Spinoza believed nature does not have a specific bearing and God is not in charge of controlling the cosmic episodes. This contrast led Long to state that should the Stoics have denied the existence of a divinely structured providence, as Spinoza did, the constant criticisms and condemnation that Stoicism received from its early days would not have happened. In a way, Spinoza tried to upgrade Stoicism to fit the modern world. He would not have been wrong as more efforts are geared toward the same purpose these days.

In conclusion, an evident relationship exists between Kant and the Stoics, especially in their ideas concerning duty, which is more important than the concise results of steps that humans have initially taken. Even the differences between them are quite intriguing. Long explained that Kant came up with his notions through a priori form of reasoning, while the Stoics employed an empiricist and naturalistic approach.

CHAPTER 4: ZENO'S STOICISM

Zeno was a Hellenistic rationalist born in Citium, a region in Cyprus. His line of descent can be traced to Phoenicia. Zeno is widely known as having founded Stoicism as a philosophical school, and he taught its tenets in Athens for many years. With a cue from the moral notions of the Cynics, the Stoic philosophy emphasized being good and generated inward peace through one's virtuous life, which should be in line with nature.

ZENO'S PHILOSOPHY

In line with the notions of the Academics, Zeno classified his philosophical ideas into three categories. The first is Logic. This encompasses many aspects, such as grammar, notions of perception, and rhetoric, among others. The second category, Physics, not only dwelled on science but entailed the nature of the universe. Ethics was the last classification of Zeno's philosophical ideas. It entailed the ultimate aim of deriving happiness by living according to nature's provisions and principles. Because Zeno's notions were subsequently broadened by other Stoic philosophers, Zeno's teachings are somewhat difficult to distinguish. Some of his notable ideas will be discussed in the following paragraphs.

ZENO'S LOGIC

In his approach to Logic, Zeno followed the ideas of some Megarians and Stilpo. He advocated the importance of constructing a structure for Logic because he felt that a man of wisdom should be able to discern a deceptive act or saying. However, Cicero emphasized that Zeno's approach to Logic is a substandard version of what was practiced by philosophers before him. This was also highlighted through the effective and practicable approach subsequently postulated by Stoics after Zeno. Chrysippus' Logic is a great example. (This will be examined in another chapter.)

Zeno classified genuine ideas into two parts: those that are understandable and those that are not. This implies that giving consent to impressions is largely through free will. Zeno explained that there are four stages leading to the genuine acquisition of knowledge. He illustrated this idea with a flat, stretched hand and a steady folding of the fist. He took out his hand and revealed his palm. He then exclaimed, "Perception is a thing like this." he folded his palm a bit and said, "Assent is like this." he then tightened his fist and explained that understanding was similar to the position of his hand. At that point, he gave the stage a name: katalepsis. He then used his left hand to grip the fist he had made on his right hand and named the stage "knowledge," which only a wise individual can possess.

ZENO'S PHYSICS

According to Zeno's beliefs, the entire universe is God Himself. The universe is a rational being whose parts are permanently attached. Within this pantheist notion, Zeno employed Heraclitus' Physics tenets, which stipulate that the entire world has an all-knowing spirit that knows all things before they occur. It is this same being that is responsible for the production of all things. Zeno explained that nature is a phenomenon that operates like an artistic fire radiating through fixed channels.

He explained, "It is the main function of art to create and produce, and what the hand accomplishes in the production of art is accomplished much more artistically by nature" – in other words, through an artistic fire which happens to be greater than any other form of art. The God-like fire (aether) stands as the foundation for all the events in the world and functions through a rather passive physical substance that does not appreciate or depreciate. The basic substance of the world emanates from fire, advances into the level of air and turns partly into water, with thicker parts turning into earth and lighter parts turning into air once more. Afterwards, it becomes fire again.

Zeno believed every living soul is a part of this same fire which becomes a single soul of the whole universe. In line with Heraclitus's notion, Zeno believed the universe has passed through constant revolutions of structuring, destruction, and restructuring. The universe is designed to ensure that only the right things occur. It prevents anything it deems wrong. All its activities are perceived as being permanently fated and will occur at will.

ZENO'S ETHICS

Zeno was perceived as a Nuremberg Chronicle's scholar. As did the Cynics, he identified just one true good everyone had to achieve. He stressed that happiness means a good life and can come to pass only with the help of the correlation of correct reason and the Logos – the universal reason which rules all things. Zeno expressed that pathos – a negative feeling – disturbs one's mind and is unpleasant and irritating to reason. It is equally contradictory to the dictates of nature. A consistent mind – from which develop activities or practices considered morally good – is a virtuous one. Genuine good is found only in virtue.

In contrast to the Cynics' ideas, Zeno had the belief that some things could be valuable, despite the fact that they are morally indifferent. He stressed that some things are relatively valuable in the ways they assist the innate human intuition of self-protection. With this, Zeno introduced the idea of "fitting action." Self-protection and those things that aid the technique are all considered valuable on a conditional basis. None of it fosters happiness, as happiness comes about only as a result of moral practices.

Furthermore, as virtue can be practiced only through good reasoning, vice can come to life only when one rejects good reasoning. This means vice and virtue are contradictory and the two attributes cannot co-exist in an agent. They can be neither added to nor subtracted from. A particular action cannot be more virtuous than others. We either act appropriately or otherwise because our feelings and desires emanate from free will. Feelings that do not exhibit good reasoning or any mental states that are passive are not moral in any form. They end up producing acts that are largely immoral. Zeno was the first to outline the four unpleasant emotions of pleasure, fear, pain, and desire (hedone, phobos, lupe, and epithumia, respectively). He is also known for having posited the three pleasant emotions of caution, happiness, and inner will, without any reasonable comparison for pain. Zeno emphasized that all negativity should be expelled completely, not just brushed aside. It should then be substituted for correct reason.

CHAPTER 5: CHRYSIPPUS' STOICISM

Chrysippus was a Stoic philosopher of Greek descent. His native town was Soli; hence, he was popularly referred to as Chrysippus of Soli. At an early age, he relocated to Athens and enrolled as a student in the Stoic school under Cleanthes. After Cleanthes' demise, Chrysippus assumed the role of the school's leader making him the third head in the school's lineage. Chrysippus' writings were prolific, and he broadened many of Zeno's important principles. Chrysippus' important ideas are pneuma and the systemization of Stoicism. His works were influenced by earlier philosophers such as Cleanthes, Zeno of Citium, Philo, Aristotle, Plato, and Diodorus.

He successfully explored Ethics, the concept of knowledge, Physics, and Logic. Chrysippus was solely responsible for the creation of Propositional Logic, which gave him a good understanding of how the universe works as well as the responsibilities of all human beings who exist in it. Chrysippus stuck strictly to the idea that fate is unchangeable, although he advocated the need for individual freedom on issues of action and thought. He also believed Ethics relies on a grasp of the world's structure. Chrysippus offered some explanations and guidelines on ways to completely eradicate some passions that seem uncontrollable but then lead to depression and, ultimately, the damage of one's soul. His contributions not only made him an influential figure but also marked the beginning of Stoicism's success as a philosophical field of study in the Roman and Greek worlds.

CHRYSIPPUS' PHILOSOPHY

During his reign, Chrysippus was successful in his constant and persistent repulsion of criticisms from the Academy. His dedication to counter every form of negative comment about Stoicism was not just to eradicate the misconstrued labeling that Stoicism had received in the past. It was also intended to ensure that future negative criticisms would be minimal. Chrysippus combined the teachings of Cleanthes and Zeno and blended them to create what was later seen as a defined Stoicism system. He created a comprehensive understanding of the practical ideas of the Stoics, as well as their concept of knowledge. Furthermore, Chrysippus is responsible for the creation of Stoicism's formal Logic. He laid the foundation for the existing structure of Stoicism. The common expression "If it weren't for Chrysippus, Stoa would not have existed" is not an exaggeration.

CHRYSIPPUS' LOGIC

Chrysippus wrote much about Logic. This is evident in the creation of his Propositional Logic. Before then, Aristotle's Logic was explained by establishing that terms such as "Socrates" and "Man" are interrelated, while Logic in Stoicism was concerned with the interrelation of terms such as "day" and "light." Philo and Diodorus Cronus (Dialecticians), Eudemus and Theophrastus (Aristotle's students) had all worked on the aforementioned syllogisms. Chrysippus was the one who appropriated the principles to blend them smoothly into a sensible structure of Propositional Logic.

PROPOSITIONS

According to Chrysippus, a proposition is an idea that has the ability to validate as well as discredit itself. He gave some instances like, "Dion is walking" and "It is day." Chrysippus noted that propositions could be simple or non-simple, and highlighted differences between the two groups. Today, the distinction is widely referred to as atomic and molecular propositions, respectively. Simple propositions are basic statements like "It is day." They are usually connected to one another to create propositions that are not simple (that is, the non-simple ones) through some logical words or connectives. This prompted Chrysippus to examine some types of non-simple or molecular propositions which are recognized in contemporary Logic. They include the conditional, the disjunction, and the conjunction. He also examined their relations to truth.

CONDITIONAL PROPOSITION

The foremost Logic-centered philosophers to examine the structure of conditional statements were Philo and Diodorus Cronus. A few centuries later, Sextus Empiricus brought their arguments to the fore.

According to Philo, conditional statements are generally truthful, apart from those that have an incorrect consequent when their antecedents are otherwise correct. This implies that the statement, "If it is night, then I am shouting" is correct unless the person becomes mute when it is night. Diodorus emphasized that a genuine conditional statement is one whose antecedent cannot, on any occasion, result in a false outcome. This renders the statement, "If it is night, then I am shouting" invalid because it can be an untrue proposition. However, it is very realistic to have contradictory propositions, as in, "If atomic parts of a thing are not in existence, atomic parts are still in existence."

Chrysippus' interpretations were strict when it came to conditional propositions. The contradictions, as explained above, are relatively impossible according to Chrysippus. He believed a conditional proposition could be true only when the logical incompatibility of the antecedent is a direct result of the consequent's denial.

CHRYSIPPUS' SYLLOGISTIC SYSTEM

Chrysippus created a pattern of deduction through the employment of five basic types of argument processes regarded as Indemonstrable Syllogisms. These assumed the positions or functions of four inference guidelines and axioms called Themata, through which syllogisms that are rather difficult in nature can be categorized under guidelines or principles.

Of the four outlined inference guidelines, only two are in use. One of the duos was known as the first Thema and happened to be a tenet of antilogism. The other one was known as the third Thema and happened to be a tenet through which strings of syllogisms could be condensed into rather simple ones. The reason for syllogism in Stoicism was not just about the creation of formal structures. Syllogism was seen a branch of study that dealt with the process of reason – that is, the "divine reason" that rules the entire world, one of which human beings are part. The main aim was looking for viable guides for inferences as well as different patterns of facts that could help human beings navigate their interactions and paths in the world.

OTHER LOGICAL EXAMINATIONS BY CHRYSIPPUS

Chrysippus analyzed ways to treat terminologies, speeches, and names correctly. He constantly spoke and wrote against contrasting and fallacious statements or views. Diogenes Laertius mentioned that Chrysippus was the author of 12 writings in a book on paradox and nine in 26 pieces on conundrums. On amphiboly, Chrysippus was responsible for seven writings in 17 books.

The significance of his choice remains unclear. Chrysippus constantly used two of the four Stoic categories: quality and substance. Later, Chrysippus was popularly known as being one of the earliest Logicians in Greece. At one time, Clement of Alexandria had made some comparisons using Homer's importance among poets. He then named Chrysippus as being on the same level among Logicians implying that he was the master of Logic in place of the almighty Aristotle. Diogenes once wrote that Chrysippus' ideas would have been most preferred had it been the gods' used dialectic. Eventually, his contributions were ignored and relegated to the background, partially because they weren't as practical as those of Aristotle. The latter's works subsequently became the widely accepted ones.

In the 19th Century, the treatment that Stoic Logic received was by no means favorable, as it became completely unproductive. It was also seen as a mere replacement of Aristotle's Logic with the use of different terms. The 20th Century brought the field to the fore once again. Then, propositional calculus and improvements in the study of Logic accorded importance to the discipline of Stoic Logic.

CHRYSIPPUS' EPISTEMOLOGY

According to the Stoics, only The Sage can identify or separate a truthful notion from an untrue one. Chrysippus had an empirical approach to his concept of knowledge. He believed human sense transfers information from the outward environment. The description of the information is conducted through a comparison with earlier deciphered information in the human mind. Zeno had explained that the impressions of senses are impressions in the souls of human beings. Cleanthes, too, had likened an impression on one's soul to the impression a seal makes on wax. Chrysippus called it a change in one's soul. This means in the same way air gets several hits whenever people speak simultaneously, one's soul is modified through all the things with which it comes into contact. The human soul is usually in a passive mood when it receives an impression. Subsequently, the impression would reveal itself as well as what caused it. A human being's ability to create such an impression, description, or name depends on what the individual has been able to understand about it. Hence, the impression must exist before a proper understanding can be achieved.

The separation of false and true presentations is done through comparison and classification as well as the use of one's memory. With human beings lies the ability to give consent, hold onto it, or withdraw it. However, the clarity and distinct appearance of a presentation can, in a way, enforce human consent as it would have been heard or seen. Therefore, if human beings are considered rational, "reason" is coined from this.

PHYSICS

Chrysippus emphasized the natural unity between things in the universe. He also argued that all parts of these things are connected and mutually dependent. He once stated that the world is a soul and controls itself. Just as Zeno stated, Chrysippus had the notion that the primitive particle of the world is fiery breath. He stressed that things are created from immovable substances and a soul. Pneuma is then responsible for giving shape to the substances, spreading through them, managing unity in the world, and constituting the soul, the spirit, and immortal parts of human beings.

According to Chrysippus, the classical elements can transform from one to the other through a process known as rarefaction and condensation. He explained that fire initially turns into solid air, air changes to water and eventually, water transforms into earth. A direct reversal of this procedure will bring about dissolution.

Chrysippus split the human soul into parts numbering eight. These are the power of speech, that of reproduction, a part he called the ruling par – situated in the human chest, and all the five senses. Chrysippus explained that the souls of humans who are very clever or wise would live beyond their physical existence. At the time, it was believed that souls perish. He opined that no soul could exist after the occurrence of a conflagration – a periodic occurrence that renews the world.

FATE

Chrysippus emphasized that every event can be attributed to fate. This means unplanned occurrences usually have inherent causes. He explained that the conformity of the universe is structured in a chronological manner, such that one cause leads to another. Hence, nothing happens without a good cause. Chrysippus believed a proposition could be true or untrue, and the status of any proposition must also be relevant in the future. Chrysippus also explained that current situations are answerable to earlier causes; hence, nothing escapes fate.

Fate, to the Stoics, is centered on the idea that the entire world is one piece. People and things can be considered dependent only on that singular piece. All things from all angles are ascertained through this relationship. In turn, the overall order of the universe shapes the interaction or relationship.

Those who hold opposing views may believe that because all

things have been predetermined and nothing can come in the way of fate, no form of individual responsibility can exist. Chrysippus tried to counter this assertion by explaining that there is indeed a difference between a difficult and simple predestination for human beings. He asserted that anything that occurs after sickness might be a function of fate. However, if an individual's healing is connected to the intervention of a physician, the intervention of the doctor was aligned with the individual's recovery by fate. Hence, the fact becomes complicated.

In general, Chrysippus believed human destiny is dependent on its interaction with things. He expressed that occasions are "co-fated" to happen. That is, the durability of cloth is not just because of fate; rather, it is co-fated to the user's ability to take care of it. An individual's escape from his enemies is co-fated with his ability to run away from them. Again, Chrysippus believed human reproduction is co-fated with the ability and willingness to engage in sexual intercourse with a member of the opposite sex because a good number of things cannot happen if the willingness is absent. Such persons must strive eagerly as individual contributions have a role to play in the actualization of fate. He stated that those contributions would be within the person's fate-provided capability.

Therefore, human actions have been determined by the time they occur and have been synced smoothly with fate. However, humans are solely responsible for the manner in which they react to some impressions. A superseding power is inherent in everything and everyone, be it irrational or rational beings or objects. All actions are direct results of cooperation among their causes. This depends on the structure of things, as well as the attributes of the agents. The only way to classify human actions as involuntary is if they occurred as a result of external causes with no contribution whatsoever from the individual's inner will.

Chrysippus believed virtue and vice are occurrences within human beings' reach and they are responsible for whichever they put into practice. He stressed that moral responsibility is a result of the freedom of willingness, and everything that comes from one's will is his or hers without considering the possibility of being able to behave otherwise. This idea of equating human responsibility with determinism is called compatibilism.

DIVINATION

In Ancient Greece, divination was called Cleromancy. Chrysippus assumed that divination was a component of the causal structure of a human being's fate. He emphasized the truthfulness of fate with the use of the idea of divination. He stressed that ample proof exists for his assertion because diviners themselves would not be able to make predictions about future events had such events occurred accidentally. According to him, signs of some events are naturally revealed through portents and omens. Chrysippus opined that despite the numerous signs concerning providence, humans have been able to know only some fragments.

GOD

Stoics had the opinion that the world itself is God. Chrysippus agreed with this and added that the world is an outpouring of God's soul. He believed that this assertion remains the principle guiding everyone and everything in the world. Chrysippus explained that the principle operates in one's mind and also embraces everything that exists. Max Weinstein subsequently called Chrysippus a pandeist for holding such beliefs.

Chrysippus tried to reveal God's existence by offering a teleological explanation. He stated that if there were a thing human beings could not possibly make, whatever made such a thing must be better than humans. He asserted that because things such as heavenly bodies are not what any human can make, the creature that produced them has a level of superiority. According to him, no one fits that description apart from God. Hence, the existence of God is real. In his descriptions, Chrysippus used God and gods interchangeably. He wrote that the ancient Greek gods could be likened to the numerous distinct parts of a singular reality. Cicero mentioned that Chrysippus equated aether to Zeus and that Poseidon is the same as the air that blows throughout the sea. Chrysippus also perceived the earth as what is known as Demeter. He named all the gods by comparing them to other things. Finally, he stated that the universal God had created the world for His own benefits.

THEODICY

Responding to an inquisition about the reason evil exists in a supposedly good world, Chrysippus stated that it is impossible to eradicate evil from the world. Moreover, it is not proper to try to eradicate it. Like Plato, he stressed that the existence of good with no evil is not possible. If there were no case of injustice, then justice or justifiable procedures would not be known. Courage wouldn't exist without cowardice, and there wouldn't be anything called foolishness if wisdom had not been put in place. Finally, temperance would not have been discovered if no one lacked it.

Furthermore, Chrysippus argued that evils exist due to the goodness of nature. Importance is attached to the fact that humans have skulls built with thin bones. This is because of utility as seen in the scenario of being hit there.

Another side of Chrysippus' argument on evils is that they are spread rationally by the dictates of Zeus. This could be because of some people's wickedness or their importance in maintaining order in the world. Therefore, evil is a disguised good in a way, and it produces the best outcome in the end. In a comic piece, Chrysippus compared evil and "coarse jest." He explained that although the jest seemed offensive in a way, it added to the meaning and relevance of the piece altogether. Hence, evil is somewhat useful.

ETHICS

Chrysippus referred to Medea as a good instance of the possibility of growing passions that are not rational due to some bad judgments. On Ethics, he emphasized that Physics is a strong facilitator of Ethics.

Chrysippus mentioned that apart from taking a cue from the nature of things and the organization or structure of the world, there are no better ways to appraise the issue of good and evil as it relates to happiness and virtue. Chrysippus stated that the principal aim in life is for human beings to live according to their individual experiences or interactions with nature. An individual's personal nature is a component of the universal nature. One should live and exist in alignment with one's nature and with that which the universe has provided. Chrysippus believed Ethics is in the nature of human beings, which is similar to the divine one generated from the aether. He stressed that the aether is a perfect representation of reason albeit materialistic and human beings should act accordingly.

Chrysippus emphasized that humans are free from desires,

such as riches, hierarchy, domination, lust and so on, which he considers irrational. Human freedom extends to humans' ability to bring their wills to reason. Chrysippus believed the highest test for any human being is that of his or her worth, dignity, and willpower.

On the issue of things that the Stoics had classified as "indifferent," Chrysippus agreed that it was acceptable in basic use to call the indifferent things which are preferred "good," but a knowledgeable individual already makes use of those things without asking. Habit and continuous practices are very important in perfecting virtue in human beings. Morals are progressive, and human beings' characters can also be improved.

In line with the Stoics' view of human beings having the ability to do without questionable emotions that contradict nature and impair good judgment, Chrysippus authored a piece on emotional therapy. He described passion as a disease that causes depression and ultimately crushes the human soul – hence, the need to remove it. Passions can be a result of bad judgments that have been allowed to generate their own inspirations. As seen in a situation in which an individual finds it difficult to halt his or her pace once they begin to run, it is impossible for humans to remove their emotions when they are in love or extremely angry. It is then important to always make advanced preparations and deal with one's inward emotions like they are of a physical nature. In conclusion, if human beings employ reason to emotions like pride, lust, or greed, such individuals will ultimately comprehend the dangers those emotions pose.

CHAPTER 6: THE STOIC PRACTICES OF MARCUS AURELIUS

Marcus Aurelius, the Emperor of Rome in 200 CE, was a staunch Stoic. His book, Private Meditations (written in Greek), gives other Stoicism enthusiasts a good avenue for learning how a man with the status of an emperor was able to live the supposed Stoic life, which is expected to be based entirely on virtue. Stoicism preaches that vice is not acceptable and many of the activities in which human beings engage are "indifferent." No doubt, Aurelius faced challenges that can be said to be as practical as much as philosophical. An understanding of his struggles helps increase scholars' knowledge of philosophy.

CONTRIBUTIONS

Being an heir, Aurelius studied philosophy and rhetoric comprehensively. The later parts of his military expeditions as an emperor prompted him to write his renowned book Meditations. However, his works were not limited to books. There were official letters, correspondence (including the one he had with Fronto, his rhetoric teacher, and friend), edicts, and others.

Aurelius' personal correspondence began before he reached the age of 20 and did not stop when he ascended to the throne. The contents were basically rhetoric on topics such as the praises of sleep, dust, and smoke. He also wrote about the value rhetoric adds to philosophy. He constantly penned personal writings, documenting births and deaths in his family, and cases of illness.

However, Aurelius' primary influence on philosophy revolves around Stoicism. In the Meditations, he recognized the efforts of his teacher, Rusticus, who gave him Epictetus' piece to read. In the letter Aurelius sent to Fronto, he acknowledged that he found extreme happiness in the explanations of the Stoic Aristo. Aurelius mentioned that afterward he became wary about his personal inadequacies and declared that he would never argue a single question from two angles – a practice he had earlier learned from his study of rhetoric. Despite the influence of Stoicism, Aurelius, like Seneca, still used the quote from Epicurus when it came to issues of Ethics. Moreover, he employed quotes from renowned philosophers such as Democritus, Heraclitus, Epictetus, Chrysippus, Plato, Antisthenes, and Homer.

INSIGHTS FROM THE MEDITATIONS

Aurelius' Meditations is a book with a distinct approach that separates it from other ancient philosophical writings. Its first part explores his recognition of and praise for the scholars and philosophers who helped shape his life in the application of knowledge, lesson derivation, inculcation of virtue, and many others. Other parts of the Meditations did not have a specific progression. His comprehensive ideas blend smoothly into each other, and inferences are drawn from different parts of the text at different intervals. Readers cannot detect the breaks in Aurelius' thoughts other than through the chapters. He constantly readdressed issues which were likely to have been a result of personal experiences. Some of these are his displeasure with the faulty living of his associates and the inevitability of death. Other recurring inquisitions in his texts, the comprehensive depiction of his imaginations, and the fact that one can extract sentences that have complete meanings from the Meditations gave Aurelius the status of a reputable philosopher.

Should a reader seek to grasp Aurelius' thoughts in one piece, he or she may tend to experience frustration as his writings can be somewhat complex and contradictory for the average reader. A philosophical appraisal of Aurelius' texts requires a specialized approach. A notable appraisal is that of Hadot (1998), who arranged Aurelius' submissions along Epictetus' principles of assent, desire, and impulse. Hadot explained that these principles are represented by Aurelius as guidelines for the application of discretion when judging others, having contentment in regards to any occurrence and, finally, correctly adjusting toward other human beings.

A reader with a philosophical mind or inclination stands to gain a lot from Aurelius' Meditations. One must know what sort of text it is. Themistius happened to be the first philosopher in the ancient world to offer a concise description of the text. He called it Aurelius' Precepts. Thereafter, a dictionary by Suidas referred to it as the leading Agoge. Aethas, a bishop, referred to it as Taeis heauton, which translates to "the writing to oneself."

In general, scholars have come to agree that Aurelius' writings – the Meditations especially – were originally written for his personal moral improvement. They also served as reminders about what he should stand for as well as the representation of the Stoic principles he strove to embody, some of which are: the notion that the world is ruled by Providence; the idea that human beings should not be irritated by the actions of their friends or colleagues but instead see those people as products of the single God; and that there is abundant happiness in practicing virtue.

The only other notable Stoic writing that explored these sorts of ideas is that of Epictetus, who offered extensive explanations for handling or responding to problems that human beings face. He stressed that the goal of reading or writing is to achieve moral development.

This idea of preparing mentally for things that have yet to occur is depicted in some slogans in the Meditations, such as not doing anything randomly, doing without impressions, and having the knowledge that some humans would inevitably be buried soon enough. Aurelius stated that anyone able to digest even the minutest aspect of such principles would be absolutely free from any fear or pain that may come his or her way.

Aurelius mentioned his study of "hupomnemasin," an Epictetus text which informed the reasons behind Aurelius' refusal to specifically reveal occurrences in his life in ways such that others would easily learn about them. The Meditations examined the reasons for Aurelius' intentional use of Stoic terms without providing clarifications. It unraveled the reason Aurelius adopted different notions of other philosophers without paying attention to their agreement or disagreement with the principles of Stoicism.

More importantly, the Meditations guide readers to search for the mistakes against which Aurelius fought as well as the acceptable habits he ultimately tried to encourage any time he discussed some principles or teachings either from the Stoic discipline or others. For instance, section XI.18 of the text, which began with the notion that all humans are in the universe for the sake of one another. The metaphysical aspect can be regarded as nature as well as atoms. It describes ten rules to be used for anger management. Section IX.28 of the text explains the Stoic principle of the repetition of eternal occurrences which helps to remind humans of mortality.

This means the approach toward studying the Meditations should be therapeutic in nature, even though it is filled with adopted assertions from different philosophers. Readers should seek to know the psychological implications of Aurelius' statements and to master the fact that Aurelius' use of "d" does not necessarily depict his conviction about it. The subsequent paragraphs will examine Aurelius' ideas and perception of how human beings can strive to live Stoically. This will be discussed with the assistance of insights from Hadot.

STOIC LIVING

Aurelius stated that he merely tried to act and live like a philosopher who puts Stoicism into constant practice. He explained this by picturing his reader as a third person who did not have the ability to live as a philosopher because of his youthful years. He mentioned that it was obvious to that individual that he was nowhere near the practice of philosophy. Hence, the individual is forced into a state of confusion. Aurelius asserted that attaining the position of a reputable philosopher was no small feat for such a person. He advised that because such a person has seen where his or her faults lie, the correct step is to ignore trying to be reputable, to lead a life of contentment; he or she should subject his or her life to the will of nature. The individual should examine what nature has in store for him or her and ensure no form of distraction exists.

Aurelius emphasized that because human beings' experiences give them a clue as to the extent to which they have lived incorrectly. They could realize that wealth, enjoyment, and reputation do not equate to a good life. He then mentioned that a worthy life entails acting according to the dictates of nature. He emphasized that in order to live this way, humans must adopt a principle through which their actions and wishes are projected. Such principles are those that revolve around evils and goods; a good human being must be courageous, just, full of temperance, and, ultimately, free.

As he expected to become an ideal Stoic, Aurelius encouraged himself to act according to the dictates of nature. A genuine practice meant he had to humble himself completely. He asked himself what nature revealed concerning his will. The aforementioned assertions seek to describe how human beings can align themselves with nature. That is, human beings must reshuffle the good or bad things that would naturally invoke certain responses and actions. According to Aurelius, the adjustment will be accomplished if human beings accept that pleasure is evil. They will immediately become angry about those pleasures experienced by the evil ones, and the pains endured by those who live virtuous lives. If human beings become angry over such things, they would simply start looking for the shortcomings of nature and become disrespectful.

He emphasized that untrue notions about what is good and what is not deny human beings the ability to act according to what nature dictates. Removal is not enough to make human beings live virtuously and act as they should, as the supposed pleasure and pain are neither completely good nor completely bad.

Seneca, a 100 CE philosopher, emphasized the importance of a comprehensive guide concerning some situations that occur even after the removal of untrue opinions and vices. He stressed that human beings would still not have an idea of what to do, or of how to do it. Seneca believed it isn't only passion that denies human beings the ability to learn about what to do in some situations; rather, inexperience is an equally important factor. Furthermore, he explained that nature does not always tell human beings the specific steps or actions to take in all cases.

Aurelius, on the other hand, believed all situations present a virtue-oriented option that human beings can always adopt. Such options are the correct actions to take. One can say that Aurelius believed virtue is not produced through the things that constitute human beings' actions. Virtue is produced through the human thoughts that accompany such actions. The question, then, is: What could those thoughts be? Should virtue possess any components at all? Believing that a virtuous life is the only good that exists isn't completely convincing.

DELIBERATION ON THE PROBLEM OF CONTENT IN STOICISM

An insight into Stoicism reveals that people who strive to be Stoics will inevitably encounter difficulties ascertaining the constituent of Stoic recommendations. Stoicism postulates that only a virtuous life is good, that vices are the only forms of evil, and that all other things that do not come under the two classifications are "indifferents." This means virtue is the only way to achieve genuine joy, while vices would only bring sadness to humans. A lack of health, reputation, or riches cannot be considered bad because they are not responsible for human beings' sadness. Fame and wealth cannot be considered good things because they cannot really make human beings happy.

The question is how can human beings act appropriately? What basis should one use for his or her choices so that they would be perceived as rational? The theoretical response would be that some things are preferred, even among the indifferents, because they align with nature in some ways. The evenness or oddness of the number of stars in the sky and the strands of hair on a human head are indifferents. What human beings naturally prefer are good health, wealth, and fame.

The Stoic principle of the things to do – that is, what one's actions should contain – is acting in alignment with nature. Cleanthes' prescription for happiness is having a life that agrees with nature. For Chrysippus, it is having a life that aligns with the dictates of the things that have occurred by nature. He believed that when humans align with nature, they carry out appropriate actions.

Aurelius believed an acceptable action is that which can be reasonably justified. However, an action cannot be considered virtuous unless it is carried out in a stable and wise manner by an individual who possesses virtue. Adequate and morally acceptable actions may not be distinguished through their components, but the mental balance of the doer differentiates the two categories.

Most often, writings that describe the adequate or correct actions of human beings ignore some important questions, such as whether it is possible to have more than a single correct action that could be carried out in a particular situation. Is the idea of justification that is considered reasonable the same as what the law specifies as reasonable individual or reasonable doubts? Can a correct action be said to be a virtuous act without a virtuous mind?

Epictetus documented Chrysippus' statement about having an impulse if he had known that he was destined to be sick. The statement expresses that because he was not aware of being destined to be sick, the correct action he should opt for is to choose good health. However, if he was actually destined to be sick, does it mean that opting for health as well as sickness would be the correct actions to take in that instance?

Diogenes documented the difference between correct actions that usually do not have anything to do with surrounding circumstances, like finding sensory organs, health, and those actions considered correct on only some occasions, such as purposely causing an affliction to one's body. The question is: Would it mean that selecting health is correct at all times, the alternatives and consequences notwithstanding?

Most scholars believe that correct actions are those that are in alignment with nature and that would naturally be chosen by any virtuous individual. Brennan (1996) posited that there could be only one correct action in any given situation. Selecting what is preferred, which ultimately aligns with nature, is only basically correct. Ideal justification is the reasoning a virtuous individual is able to come up with. Chrysippus' assertion that an adequately virtuous individual carries out every correct action leaving out nothing, would be untrue should there be many correct actions for a situation. The constraint is that leading a Stoic life may mean an individual should have the ability to mention that some small actions are to be chosen as preferred indifferents. However, the citations appear to speak only on the sorts of actions human beings must take.

Brennan and Barney shared an insight into the possibility that Stoicism could lead an individual to make good use of their respective preferred indifferents and also identify the contradiction between that and the forms of virtuous character in which a proper Stoic should be involved – for instance, giving up his or her life for the sake of his or her nation.

Brennan, in a bid to offer an adequate description of the Stoic teaching that individuals must give their best to their country instead of themselves, employed the use of the oikeiôsis guidelines that explain that humans have an innate likelihood of caring for one another. The first set being one's immediate family, friends, community members, and other human beings across the world. Although this likelihood might not be sufficient to overshadow self-interest in human beings, Brennan posited that the Stoic idea that indifferents cannot help achieve happiness gets in the way of justifiable deliberations. This is because Stoics would desire the indifferents had they been good. Because they are not, Stoics then moved toward considering a way to classify them according to the dictates of justice.

This consideration does not in any way tamper with the Stoics' take on virtue. Rather, the Stoics consider their immediate environment's utilities, as well as its take on the rights of property to validate or give substance to its "dictates of justice."

Aurelius' mode of examining issues of content in Stoicism is similar to that of Cicero's. That is, the classification of appropriate conduct emanates from notions concerning the dictates of justice, but the content of justice does not originate from Ethics. Aurelius believed the content of justice originated from the notion that the cosmos is a nation in which every rational individual is a citizen. The responsibilities of these citizens come with specific expected acts.

Aurelius opined that individuals should be bothered by just two things. These are the love he or she has and having just behavior. He stated that having just behavior means having a communal behavior. That is, individuals should live the way true citizens would in the cosmic nation as everyone has a part to play toward its welfare. Those who do not participate in communal activities can be likened to the enemy of the nation and, as such, would ultimately break the nation.

Aurelius classified the communal activities as indifferents and not as a virtue. This means he believed individuals should strive to achieve preferred indifferents for their entire community because the goals or desires of the community and its dwellers cannot contrast. Aurelius emphasized that the desires he mentioned are the common things sought after in a community. For instance, although hunger is not classified as evil and food is not classified as good, a Stoic would nonetheless tackle hunger in another individual by providing food instead of telling the person that hunger is not evil and food is not good. This is because human beings have innate concerns for each other, a habit common to parents as they cater to their offspring. Aurelius emphasized one should see other human beings as oneself when thinking about ways to assist them and ways to avoid causing them harm.

Aurelius expressed the notion that strong desires channeled toward a communal benefit represents a good example of being rational. He also stated that human beings must act according to constitutions because communalism is a crucial factor in the institution of any constitution. Aurelius believed human beings are responsible for perfecting political setups; therefore, their actions must align with positive political lives.

In conclusion, Aurelius negated the idea that a contradiction exists between an individual's good and that of his or her nation. He stressed that the nation as a whole has a nature of good things. Whatever is not a hazard to the nation cannot bring harm to those who live in it. He also said that the individuals who are part of the nation are the determinants of stability, perfection, and good living conditions. Aurelius compared the relationship between the nation and the rational individuals living in it using the cooperation that exists between the body and its limbs. This comparison dates back to the Republican era of Plato. It entails the fact that damage or injury to an individual residing in a nation is tantamount to damage or injury to others and, ultimately, the entirety of the nation. For Plato, it is very important that stakeholders form opinions and arrive at decisions with one voice. Aurelius, however, stressed the need for every individual to carry out his or her specific functions accordingly, as everything forms the nation. This, to him, is necessary because a limb cannot be without its complete part, which is the body. Individuals cannot be whom they claim they are without the nation of which they are part. In essence, Aurelius' idea of piety was formed through his beliefs about the relationship between parts and their corresponding wholes.

AURELIUS' PIETY

Aurelius noted that whenever things go well within it, nature is satisfied. Likewise, when consents are not falsely given to some impressions, all things go well rationally. When nature channels its desires to communal activities, when it inculcates passions and interests for those things within the human capability, and when it also accepts the things that have been delegated to it, all things work smoothly. That last condition explains the idea of piety. In general, piety emphasizes the notion that the cosmos and its entirety are structured through providence. Its appearance or structure cannot be better than it already is. That also means its components are already in their best form. With this background, the human habit with respect for the cosmos should exhibit conformity, as well as genuine love.

Hadot mentioned that Aurelius followed Epictetus in explaining the differences between desires and impulses. He refined his description by limiting human beings' impulses to areas of their activities. He described desire by comparing it to areas in which human beings are passive. Human beings are to have desires for anything that occurs to them. This explanation by Hadot is somewhat misleading in the sense that the Stoics believe the human response to things that happen to them can be classified as impulses, and desire is a form of impulse as well. Aurelius stressed that humans have the choice to either subdue their desires or eliminate them. Epictetus emphasized that humans should desist from desires for some time.

Aurelius' take on eliminating desires stems from the fact that humans are liable to have strong desires for the wrong things, which is dangerous, as their impulses for such things may be uncontrollable. This notion gives room to criticize his original idea of having desires for the things that happen to one. Desires should probably be equated to striving. Then, with content, human beings can accept whatever results it brings. This knowledge of piety helps shed light on Aurelius' take on atoms and providence.

ATOMS OR PROVIDENCE

At different points in the Meditations, Aurelius listed contrasting notions: nature, reason, and providence against the notion of atoms. He did not give detailed explanations of his classification, but one can deduce that he was trying to create a distinction between the notions. The first is the Stoic notion that the structure of the universe and whatever happens within it, is in line with the plan of a providential super being. The second is the Epicurean belief that the universe's structure is the result of some random collisions of atoms. It remains unclear why Aurelius laid out the contrasting notions.

One way his actions could be understood is through acknowledging that his vastness in Stoic Physics could have led him to have positive opinions toward some aspects of Physics in Epicureanism. At a point, Aurelius even declared his fear concerning his understanding of Physics. Another way to understand him is to consider his opinion that adopting a Stoic or Epicurean Physics should not stop anyone from living his or her life according to the dictates of Stoicism, such as having rational thoughts, living with a united purpose, and outliving the challenges of the usual evils and goods. A final possible reason is their opinions differ. The Stoics and Epicureans' take on Ethics converges at some point; this could have solidified Aurelius' belief in their Ethics.

In an extract, Aurelius mentioned the "Providence or atoms" notion. His intention was to create a union among the distinct takes on Ethics in different reputable schools at the time, Epicureans included. He mentioned the likes of Antisthenes, Democritus and others concerning the importance of virtue and that on which human beings naturally place the most value – that is, pain, death, reputation, and life.

Aurelius explained that the Epicurean notion of the cessation and dispersion of the human soul after death is similar to the Stoic notion that after death, humans are either transformed or extinguished. He made mention of Epicurus' quote, which explains that a gruesome pain is usually short, but human beings can bear pains that last for long periods. He seemed to be driving at the fact that irrespective of one's philosophical sentiments, one should be a slave to reputation, pain, and death. He also shared the view that human beings need not grumble, as everything is there as a result of providence. Hence, things could not have been any other way, and it is not right to complain. Even if all things have happened by chance, there is no use in grumbling.

Despite the tendencies, Aurelius did not express support for the Physics of the Epicureans. After weighing in on the "atoms or providence" notion, he constantly emphasized that the universe is under the control of a knowledgeable nature that also functions as a component, just as citizens would within a country. It is important to not read too much into Aurelius' mixed reactions over his grasp of Physics. He could have simply tried to express that his knowledge of Stoic Physics was lacking and not that he felt the Stoic Physics was in any way inferior to that of the Epicureans. He clarified that he had adequate knowledge of what a life that aligns with nature is, as well as how to live it accordingly.

Through his take on Providence, Aurelius improved on the Stoic notion that all other things apart from virtue and vice are indifferent. Because reputation, health, and wealth are randomly shared among the cruel and the virtuous, he believed it is impossible to declare such things as good as they contradict the idea of providence. His assertion was not intended to dispute the relevance of Ethics in Stoic Physics. Stoics assert that the notions of other individuals who cannot be said to be virtuous are not strong, adequate, or reliable because such persons would not possess profound knowledge. It should be known that a Stoic of Aurelius' sort would find every means to support his beliefs on Ethics. Aurelius saw this sort of argument as a defense mechanism in certain conditions where his opinions were weak.

In conclusion, Aurelius used the notion of "atoms or providence" to highlight behavior that could not be found in a pious individual.

Aurelius asked if individuals were not satisfied with the roles they had been assigned to carry out were a component of nature. He referred to the two ideas of providence and atoms and asked if anything showed that the cosmos is a nation. He explained that for humans to grasp the idea of "atoms or providence," a need exists to link the notion with personal dissatisfaction, which also points back at him. Aurelius tried to admit that he was wrong for being dissatisfied with the way things were. He was more or less addressing himself by explaining that if one perceives that the way things are isn't what it ought to be, one would believe that the situation is not a product of Providence. Because they are not products of Providence, they must have occurred randomly.

In this sense, atoms can be said to operate like the hidden will of individuals to see faults with the way things are. The idea helps lend a voice to an individual who might have complaints about the way things are. This also highlights the fact that a dispute exists between being convinced about the providential nature of the universe and being dissatisfied with everything that occurs. As soon as this dispute or contrast is identified and examined, any Stoic would have knowledge of the one for which to opt.

Aurelius explained certain processes. He stated that when regarded from the angle of Providence, the cosmos is structured similarly to a nation. This means every part is structured to help foster the whole. Aurelius had begun to think of the dual idea that the universe could be a cosmos or a mixture of confusion. However, he quickly brushed aside such thoughts by insisting that the universe is definitely a cosmos.

Yet Aurelius did not need to state that. In most cases, atoms represent impiety in this sort of situation. This means Aurelius was merely correcting his personal grumbles that impiety breeds complaints. This showed his tendency to share the sentiments of the Epicureans, even though genuine

Epicureans do not complain about the bad things that come their way as a result of a randomly operating cosmos. Instead, they lead rational lives.

The other recognized instance of the use of "atoms or providence" depicts that one must be contextual in determining anticipated results and examining the ways in which those things would yield results so as to effect some personal psychological changes. The anticipated results probably required exaggerated opinions to amend the innate probability to which he thought he could fall prey.

This should be kept in mind while one seeks to understand Aurelius' notions as a tendency exists to discover disputing opinions, contrasting views, and nervousness in his works. This could lead the reader to think he is not straightforward or that he doesn't have a mind of his own.

REMOVING IMPRESSIONS

Aurelius constantly told himself that he had to do without his impressions. The Stoic epistemology stresses that physical things in the universe have the tendency to leave an impression on both human and animal minds, just as a piece of writing would leave an impression on plain surfaces, and objects would leave an impression on wax. However, human beings have the ability to either consent to such impressions or deny them altogether. Individuals are judged based on their conformity or consent to impressions. Put simply: judgments are derived from the individual projection of human impressions. Although consent is given willingly, impressions are not structured in that manner. Humans cannot remove their impressions simply by eliminating them. What Aurelius wanted to get across is the Stoic argument with Academic Skeptics. This argument states that any wise individual would not consent to other things apart from those which perfectly depict what they genuinely feel they stand for in the world.

Hadot maintained that Aurelius implied that human beings should accept or give consent only to realistic and objective explanations of external things. Hadot explained that Aurelius was telling himself to eradicate judgments of all those things not present in his personal behavior. The differences between personal value judgments and a reliable, evident fact are found more in Existentialism than in Stoicism because value, according to the Stoics, is backed up by facts. Aurelius constantly expressed great pleasure in the soothing appearance of the whole cosmos.

Taking after Epictetus, Aurelius is correct to have emphasized the notion that human beings should desist from making judgments on what is good and what is bad because such judgments are the explanations of virtue and vice, respectively. Only a virtuous individual has such knowledge. Aurelius is also correct to have always tried to reduce the value of some things originally considered with high regard.

For instance, he wrote that the correct impression in cases of foods or delicacies is that meats from pigs, birds, or even fish are actually the corpses of such animals. In addition, the juices from drained grapes form wines, and clothes are sheep's wool that has been dipped in the extracts or blood of other creatures for its coloring. Aurelius described the process of intimacy as that which involves the unpleasant rubbing of one set of genitals against another, as well as the expulsion of irritating discharges. The enumerated impressions help one see those processes, meals, and activities for what they truly are.

Aurelius clarified that the aforementioned description shows the barest form of everything that was mentioned, as he had only divided them into smaller, more concise pieces. He then mentioned that such descriptions were enough to reduce an individual's interest in such things drastically. Aurelius' assessments of impression have another complementary standpoint. He stated that things which naturally have lesser value should be seen from a wider point of view to reveal their true advantages.

He was able to describe ways in which one could examine things from the barest angle. In an extract, he stated that the importance of a great mind is to have the ability to evaluate all the things one experiences in life in a systematic and truthful way. One must constantly reflect on them to determine their usefulness, purposes, values, and functions in the cosmos.

With that explanation, Aurelius stressed the need to contextually reintegrate all things into their appropriate cosmic structure to adequately appreciate their value. In contrast to the initial notion, the aim was not to see the things around the universe as lacking any form of value; instead, the idea was to perceive the true composition, structure, and form of all things. This is identified through careful consideration of what these things contribute to the entire universe. Describing things using their physical appearance when they are singled out from the things to which they complement is not based on their raw appearance. Rather, it is their synchronization with the intelligent and pleasant structure of the cosmos.

Aurelius stated that if some portions of a loaf of bread break open, although the openings are not by the baker's design, in a way they fit into the bread's design and ultimately arouse a consumer's cravings. Another example is the fact that some fruits are at their ripest stages when they break open. Some things are not appealing when they are singled out from their cohabiting groups, even though nature has designed them to be what they are. Hence, they inform many human decisions.

When one is to determine the things that align with the provision of nature, one must examine their functions, their roles, and the ways they contribute positively to the cosmos. Another way to identify the things that align with nature is to look at the things that occur constantly or the results from reliable samples. As soon as an individual recognizes this active participation, such a person can ascertain the values of things and how they contribute pleasantly to a perfectly structured universe.

Because an idea of the substitutes for removed impressions has been made known, it is expedient to examine the question of the exact sorts of things that should be removed and what it means to remove them. Aurelius shared an indifferent idea on impressions and judgments. He constantly told himself to remove his personal impressions and go without forming opinions. Aurelius believed he could do things that his impression considered positive or adequate and he could always endure anything his opinion considered endurable. However, it shouldn't be this way. Aurelius did not really understand the contrast between judgments and impressions. He merely followed the loose manner in which earlier Stoics and other scholars had used "impression." Epictetus, Aurelius' role model, had opined that the poem Iliad is a mere representation of impressions. Personally, Aurelius used "impression" as the construction of a standard, acceptance, the effect an individual has on another, and the angle at which a particular thing appears to individuals. These and others constitute the recognized usage of "impression." The question remains: What sorts of impressions must human beings remove?

Assistance from Plato's Protagoras would be helpful to determine this because Stoicism was widely influenced by it. Although the text highlighted and compared the effects of appearance through a measurement process that was usually incorrect, it could be used as a yardstick in identifying the shortcomings in Aurelius' idea of perspective and isolation in terms of impressions. As a form of correction, he prescribed that an individual carefully examine his or her impressions, trying them out with the help of Ethics, Dialectics, and Physics. This also means individuals should try to determine how they would fare by putting themselves up against their understanding of Dialectics, Physics, and Ethics because the three are a result of the "whole."

He stated that individuals should watch the whole all the time. They must try to determine the particular things that inform their impressions, and reverse it by identifying the causes, the shapes in which they come, and the reason for their existence. They should also ascertain the specific time at which they would be halted completely.

In regards to involuntary impressions, Aurelius' idea of "remove" may imply "replace." He could have meant that individuals should clear up some impressions for the sake of actions and responses. Rather, they should place their attention on grasping the whole, which would ultimately make such persons have others' impressions.

In a way, the Stoics' idea that the human mind is like wax on which all sorts of objects are pressed, or a sheet of paper on which a variety of things could be written, influences the notion of "removing." Aurelius tried to substitute incorrect impressions with others that could be said to have a better knowledge of reality. Indeed, achieving the latter purpose requires the complete removal of the first. This is because resisting consent from a convincing impression necessitates its replacements with another.

At one point, Aurelius stated that the character of an individual's mind could not be different from its impression. This would not be fair if impressions are not formed willingly. Aurelius might have thought impressions might have been formed unwillingly in the initial stage and would ultimately be controlled by human beings. If anyone resists consenting that riches are good, such a person would eventually stop seeing riches as being good. An individual's behavior would not likely affect his or her impressions, especially calculative impressions.

In conclusion, Aurelius' Meditations considered many varying notions. It is important to focus attention on an aspect of understanding Aurelius' ideas and the ways in which his opinions about some notions are similar to his ultimate plan of how he should live like a Stoic. It is also important to examine his statements about the idea that humans are minute components of the cosmos and that everyone dies in the end. Hence, one should lead a purposeful life instead of living like objects that are manipulated by outside forces.

CHAPTER 7: EPICTETUS' STOICISM

Epictetus was born around 50 CE in Hierapolis, a Greek community. He was a philosopher who constantly preached, taught, and practiced Stoic Ethics. He was quite popular because of his consistent advocacy, as well as the strength of his submissions on Ethics. He was also credited for his effective teaching approaches. He paid particular attention to freedom, integrity, and self-management. He developed this idea by tasking his students with an insightful analysis of two basic concepts. These two concepts were "volition" and "using impressions appropriately." As far as the tradition of morals goes, Epictetus' contributions cannot be overemphasized. In fact, he was more than an advocate for morals; his approaches, suggestions, and practices of Stoic Ethics give him a position of timeless importance.

BRIEF HISTORY AND WORKS

A considerable number of years in Epictetus' life were spent with Epaphroditus, who had a popular post in Nero's court. The exact time in which Epictetus arrived in Rome and his educational background remains uncertain. He is known to have gained some knowledge under the tutelage of Musonius Rufus, who was a senator and a staunch Stoic who occasionally taught in Rome. After Epictetus was freed from slavery, he started to teach privately but was subsequently forced to leave the community due to a ban enforced by Domitian. He later started a cultural center in Epirus, Nicopolis, and northwest Greece. He stayed at the school until he died. The documented reports in his Discourses reflect the career he eventually pursued.

The main documentation of Epictetus' thoughts is in four

standard volumes called The Discourses. The preface states that The Discourses were not penned personally by Epictetus. They were originally ghostwritten by Arrian, a historiographer, to project the importance of Epictetus' thoughts. Some scholars believe Arrian merely revised The Discourses initially compiled by Epictetus. However, no source of validation exists for the two suggestions. An abridged version of The Discourses is known as Encheiridion, meaning "a handbook" in English. It explores the submissions of Epictetus on a much smaller scale.

Epictetus' basic thoughts came from the early stages of Stoicism. He mentioned the writings of Zeno, Cleanthes, and Chrysippus. Some of these pieces are Chrysippus' On the Possible, On Choice, and On Impulse. Many aspects of these works are in alignment with Epictetus' teachings and are constantly seen in the submissions of Epictetus.

It is possible that Epictetus recognized the influences and importance of other schools of thought, the most obvious being those of Plato. Epictetus drew strength from Plato's depiction of Socrates in his short dialogs. Similarities can be seen in Plato's Gorgias, which showcases the source of Epictetus' admiration of give-and-take processes, his interest in tasking the presuppositions of a hearer, and his confidence in the things that could be derived through a good explanation of values. Another piece that must have influenced Epictetus' submissions is The Theaetetus. It is quite similar to Epictetus' thoughts on the relationship between humans and divinity, as well as the contemplative spirit possessed by humans.

IMPORTANT THINGS TO NOTE IN THE APPROACH TOWARD EPICTETUS' THOUGHTS AND PRACTICES

To have a full understanding of Epictetus' submissions, one

must be conversant with his personal aims. With reference to The Discourses, Epictetus seemed to have been a philosopher who constantly sought to enhance others' ethical practices ensuring that the expression of his personal satisfaction was brought to the fore. This implies that it is somewhat difficult to present his specific ideas. The most difficult concepts, according to Epictetus, have constantly been reviewed and interpreted in varying ways by many scholars. His decision to not express some of his thoughts, as well as the not-so-clear citations in The Discourses, means that it is not appropriate to draw any inference from his concepts. One should not assume that they are fully aware of the relationship between Epictetus' thoughts and older Greek philosophical tenets.

BASIC PHILOSOPHICAL NOTIONS

Rationality

The most prominent aspect of Epictetus' philosophical notions was his explanation of what it takes to be human. A reasonable mortal being "reasonable" (rational) simply implies that human beings can use impressions via a reflective process. Just like humans, other animals put their impressions to use. The ways in which they act are the results of the circumstances in which they must have found themselves. Human beings analyze the constituents of their impressions to ascertain whether they are correct. This ability signifies that every human has the capacity to give consent. Consent is controlled by the knowledge one has of sequential consistency or the contrast between the suggestion still being evaluated, and those notions of which one is already convinced.

If one has no knowledge of any contrasting view, one would instantly give consent, but when one senses contradictions, the probability is high that one would turn down either of the contrasting views. For instance, Morgana murdered her children because she felt it was a positive thing to do. However, if she had been given adequate explanations concerning the error in such decisions, she would not have done so. The disgust that erupts whenever one is deceived, as well as one's inability to give consent to things seemingly untrue, is Epictetus' integral explanations about humans.

Relationship with God

Epictetus found the effectively rational world setting for rationality in humans to be very important. The assurance he had in the precisely sequential nature of all things is evident through his continuous expression and references to Zeus (God) as the creator and controller of the universe. There were no instances in which he compared these powers to the powers possessed by other gods. Although he spoke about some Grecian gods, Zeus had the permanent supreme status. He finds pleasure in being accompanied, but he never needs any real aid. No one can oppose him. Epictetus perceived that Zeus is naturally, inherently, and permanently a part of nature and its phenomena. In theory, he can be reached and understood by human beings, just as other things in the universe can be understood. Through consistent trials, reasonable human beings would have the knowledge that Zeus can be an individual, a rational person whose aims and thoughts are like those of human beings. Coming to this awareness, prompts one to admire and render praises unconditionally on every occasion of one's life.

God is responsible for the creation of the human race and every other thing in the universe. He exhibits a benevolent attitude toward human beings. Human beings are rational only through God's gifts or blessings. Human beings have similar natures and feelings as God does. Epictetus expressed that the human mind is a residue of Zeus' fragments from his being. As soon as humans come to personal conclusions, we have, in a way, assigned the same authority that controls the world into use. In essence, one can conclude that God has given humans a part of his dominion.

Volition

The human ability to make choices makes one responsible for one's actions and positions. Epictetus was very interested in examining the exact meanings or results that could stem from this Stoic notion. In order to understand how he examined the concept, it is necessary to understand that "prohairesis" often implies the human ability to make choices rather than the process of choosing.

Epictetus explained that volition is unrestricted by nature. Through this, freedom, according to him, is a permanent and inherent attribute of all human beings. The idea of being able to come to decisions independently means that decisions are not influenced by any external force; they would not be seen as decisions if they were. However, human beings are indeed very capable, and so are very distinct from some other supposed higher animals that do not reflect on impressions before they act.

This power to make decisions is the genuine human within. It is the real being of any human being. Nothing else compares to one's aims, attitudes, or actions. They are simply a result of one's way of using impressions. The way one's body appears and feels, the things one possesses, the manner in which one relates to others, the favorable or unfavorable outcomes of one's projects, and one's status and recognition in the world – all are just preliminary facts concerning the individual and also the aspects of one's experience. They are not genuine attributes of the self. In fact, they exist outside the circle of volition.

Value

The difference between the things that can be considered part or not part of the circle of volition forms the fundamentals of Epictetus' notion of value. The humankind good has an aspect of volition attached to it. This aspect is the status of one's virtue, the correct practice of one's rational attributes in which one does not just behave rightly through the acquisition of knowledge, but also understands one's relationship with God, as well as experiences God's sequential arrangement and control of the world with joy. This sort of proposition is what humans can appropriately desire.

It is not inappropriate to assume that good things have numerous advantages to humans and, as such, they deserve to be pursued because that is the innate conception of good in all humans. The misappropriation is in the application of these innate conceptions – human beings believe that external things possess constant and reputable value. In the real sense, the different situations in one's life are the things with which volition must interact. On their own, they cannot be considered good or bad.

"The materials of action are indifferent, but the use we make of them is not indifferent."

There are some external phenomena far more natural to humans than others, just as one's feet are naturally considered free of dirt or stains, and just as we allow grains to keep growing rather than cutting them off. However, this occurs when we see ourselves as being independent and not part of a larger substance.

Chrysippus said, *"The foot, if it had a mind, would welcome becoming muddy for the sake of the whole. Even one's own death is of no particular concern if that is what the orderly workings of the universe require."*

This is not a warning to completely discard externals.

Epictetus explained, *"Externals must be used with care because their usage is not an indifferent matter, yet at the same time with composure and tranquility because the material being used is indifferent."*

Even with one's understanding that a particular thing does not have sufficient inherent value, one can still pursue it vigorously as long as one does so within the confinement of one's rational stance. Epictetus used the analysis of ball players who know that the ball which they persistently chase has no inherent value of its own but persist in catching it due to the value placed on participating in the game.

Adjusting Emotions

Revaluing external phenomena ushers in a great number of certainties and genuine peace. Anxiety, desires, fear, and other conditions are proceeds from the incorrect assumption that happiness can be achieved only externally. Epictetus snubbed the assumption that those conditions are consequences of one's circumstances or internal occurrences far beyond one's managerial ability. He stated that one's feelings and attitudes are the projection of the things that appear right to one – a result of one's view of value. Once one's views are adjusted, one's feelings will take a new turn.

This analogy can also be adapted to emotions, such as betrayal and anger, which are relative to the habits of others. The things others decide to do are relevant or important only to the actors themselves. To others, such things have no consequence and are completely external. Hence, one should not get angry with another individual for making bad decisions. Having pity is acceptable. However, if one has the chance, the appropriate reaction would be to assist in revealing such a person's wrongdoings. Epictetus' idea of adjusting to emotions does not preach that one should not exhibit any form of feeling and act like a statue. A very smart individual might get scared or intimidated when danger occurs without foresight, although there won't be any incorrect consent in such situations.

Nonetheless, adequate responses should be possessed. Epictetus stated, *"It is fitting to be elated at the good."* In other words, one should be happy with the good things within one's soul, and one should also have an awareness of caution whenever one is processing choices somewhat bad in nature. Being thankful to God is equally relevant to nature. As one grooms one's ethical beliefs, it is adequate to encounter the harshness of being remorseful and being an agent of ethical development.

Adequate Concern for Others

In one's interactions with other human beings, Epictetus posited that one must emulate an ideally modest attitude (aidos) and continuously express love toward the entirety of humanity. Modesty has its roots in the acknowledgment of other people's views and the decision to curb one's personal, socially unacceptable habits. Loving humanity means being willing to make efforts for others' benefit. These sorts of efforts are rendered specifically to those with whom one shares some specific roles. One's most important contribution is to assist others in growing their personal rational abilities. It is also important to support and foster the desires of the individuals with whom we are connected in one way or another.

It is not appropriate to think that having adequate feelings for one's family or friends would always make one vulnerable to weak emotions as soon as they encounter welfare problems. Epictetus opined that in the same way humans admire and love a goblet and remain calm after it is damaged due to their being aware of its fragility, humans should endeavor to be affectionate toward their wards, friends, and partners, and constantly remind themselves that every human being is mortal. The most crucial relationship is that which human beings should have with God. Human-being-to-human-being interactions should never lead to denying or rebuking God. Instead, they should help everyone remain happy and joyous about the natural universe. Being worried about others and reveling in their company is a genuine aspect of the nature of human beings.

On the other hand, an irresponsible habit is not in any way connected. A parent who stays beside a very ill child exhibits a more acceptable rational act than the parent who absconds and hides to cry.

The Human Mind and Body

Epictetus believed Zeus' overall capabilities were not unlimited. This is because he would not have been able to carry out an action that was illogical. For instance, it was impossible to have ensured that a child would have existed before the existence of his parents, and no one could have made choices outside his or her personal thoughts. Despite

God's kindness, He is unable to make the human being indestructible, just as volition is. In fact, the human body does not belong to anyone, as no one can shape the things that can occur to it. This shows that there is a clear-cut distinction between the states of one's body and mind. On several occasions, Epictetus used expressions that either ridiculed the human body or depicted it as a tool for the mind. He described the body as: *"pathetic little flesh," "cleverly molded clay"* and a *"little donkey."*

At one point, he described the human body and all possessions as "fetters" on one's mind. This expression projects the imagery of Plato's description of the body as being a prison. Nonetheless, Epictetus seemed to prefer his institution's notion concerning the mind's material structure over Plato's concept, which states that it is a distinct spiritual substance. Epictetus also described the human mind as a breath that God has placed into the sensory organs. Again, he explained that the mind could be likened to a vessel of water laden with rays.

Approach to Education

Epictetus vividly outlined the differences between the act of learning through and what can be called education for the purpose of leading a good life by learning the habits and acts that foster correct behaviors. The second form of education is of great necessity. The initial form may possess vital value, but it can turn into a stumbling block toward ethical progress if over flogged.

The fields of study present in Epictetus' school consisted of studying some philosophical texts by Stoic writers who reigned during the Hellenistic era. An instance is Chrysippus' On Impulse, as well as some pieces of Logic written by

Archedemus.

The constant mention of logical features shows that these teachings were present in the curriculum of Musonius, who was responsible for Epictetus' education in Rome. This sort of knowledge acquisition is somewhat crucial in growing one's intellectual capacity, similar to the way sportsmen introduce weights into their practices so as to train their muscles. Barnes explained that some instructions are evident in what was regarded as Physics in the ancient world.

Education for the sole purpose of living was originally self-education. It brings out the ability of self-correction – an ability that resides in our rational nature by default.
Epictetus completely snubbed the pattern of thoughts that prescribes moral improvement depends solely on assistance from God.

Epictetus explained, *"Have you not hands, fool? Has not God made them for you? Sit down now and pray your nose may not run! Wipe it, rather, and do not blame God."*

The genuine procedures to improve oneself originally involved the conscious effort of reducing the pace of one's thinking procedures to make room for reflection before one gives consent.

This process could also be translated as: *"Impression, wait for me a little. Let me see what you are and what you represent."*

As the attitude of examining one's impressions becomes more prominent, adequate reactions would start occurring spontaneously. Still, persistent monitoring is necessary to protect oneself from retrogressing. It is never advisable to depend only on habitual acts.

Concise therapeutic methods could also be important for the advancement of Ethics. Epictetus opined that his students had to completely neglect the use of the words "good" and "bad," not because these words cannot be ideally applied in the lives of human beings, but because they are often used or applied incorrectly. Therefore, the need exists to "kill" one's dislikes and desires, making use of pure, undiluted impulse. In conclusion, to suppress some personal bad attitudes, it is helpful to constantly practice the attitudes in direct contrast to the ones one seeks to suppress.

CHAPTER 8: SENECA

During the Imperial Era in Rome, Seneca was one of the country's prominent philosophers. With original pieces written in Latin, Seneca made a contribution to Stoicism that cannot be overshadowed. When it came to the literature of Stoicism, Seneca was a crucial figure at the time. To this very day, his Stoic thoughts have been adopted by many enthusiasts. His works helped resuscitate many Stoic principles during the Renaissance era and had continued to aid later Stoics to comprehend the basic principles of the philosophy adequately. Compared to the fragments that had been recorded about Stoicism before his time, Seneca's pieces show that he had vast knowledge about the philosophy as he covered many aspects extensively. Beyond that, Seneca made advancements by influencing some other philosophical schools, most significantly in his Letter and his Consolations. Seneca's writing, On Mercy, is known to be the foremost instance of a "mirrors of princes" literary work.

Although for many centuries Seneca's contribution was largely unused and snubbed, the past few decades have witnessed a sudden increased interest in them. The recent influx of appraisals is relative to the revisiting of the Roman tradition by many scholars. The clarity that has been established concerning the Hellenistic philosophical schools has also been a contributor. The recent advancement in the study of Ethics, which ultimately triggered the study of relationships, emotions, roles, and fellowship among humans, has added to the reawakening of Seneca's Stoic philosophy. In addition, Foucault's style of reading Seneca's works prompted many scholars to understand Seneca's thoughts as being relevant to modern times.

Through all the challenges he faced, Stoicism was a constant in Seneca's dealings and his life in general. Attalus, a Stoic Sage, was directly responsible for Seneca's introduction to philosophical studies. Seneca was also fascinated by the works of Cato, and he constantly made references to his works. However, Seneca did not restrict himself to the tenets of Stoicism. Even after he died, other philosophers, such as Pascal, Erasmus, and others, continued to make references to his works. Two popular instances are Nassim Taleb (a trader turned notable author who discussed the relevant contributions of Seneca in a whole paragraph in one of his recent books) and Tim Ferriss (an entrepreneur who released an audio piece on Seneca's contributions and is jokingly referred to as "Seneca" by readers of his famous blog).

Seneca's display of concrete interest does not come as a surprise. For as many pieces as he wrote on philosophical ideologies, Seneca used all to manage and direct all humans (as well as the individuals with whom he was very familiar) through the hurdles, gloom, and bloom of being wealthy. He moved away from being enormously wealthy to being an exile and subsequently managed the suicidal decree from Nero – his own student. What this sequence of events in his life preaches is that one should not be dissuaded because of one's current experiences. Rather, humans should constantly ask themselves how to ensure that such a life becomes ultimately meaningful. Seneca was able to live above riches and was also a teacher to one of history's most incapable emperors in Rome. Still, his pieces on morals constantly encouraged humans to become better individuals.

An article by Elizabeth Kolbert in The New Yorker explained that some critics, such as Robert Hughes, have labeled Seneca an insincere philosopher in the ancient period. Modern writers have posited a slightly different opinion of him.

Kohbert explained that although it is quite possible to have seen Seneca as being insincere, he actually exercised some control over morals. Seneca was very much aware of his stances. He had written that he did not consider himself a wise man and would not on any occasion become one. He was very conscious of his imperfections and so condemned plying complex routes. Seneca may have been filled with politics, authoritative positions, riches, and so on, but he wasn't short of philosophical dispositions like the examination of his personal notions or ideas and self-consciousness.

CONTRIBUTIONS

Seneca's pieces have constantly been linked to his personal experiences. This is because many of his writings showcase the healing abilities possessed by philosophical tenets – with Seneca himself being the evidence. Despite the style he adopted, his writings, on most occasions, are not a result of his direct experiences. Seneca merely used a figurative representation of himself. He treats matters that bother him in a manner that prompts his readers to reflect on such matters as they apply to their personal lives instead of Seneca's.

During the Roman Empire, Roman literature was greatly influenced by Stoic ideas, and Seneca's tragedies were crucial aspects of it all. Seneca was not a poet who tried to imbibe Stoic notions into his works; rather, he was a staunch Stoic who had chosen to write poems. One cannot ascertain the ways in which the Stoic practices of Seneca relate to his tragedies, as scholars constantly argue about the reasons a Stoic like Seneca had a flair for writing poems in the first place. At one time, some thought the two fields were authored by two different Senecas. However, the dominant ideas in Seneca's tragedies are believed to share similarities with his philosophical notions. Seneca's plays depicted his interest in Ethics. They explored his ideas on the consequences of possessing extreme emotions.

STOIC NOTIONS OF SENECA

Practicing Philosophy

Scholars who have read the philosophical works of Aristotle or Plato often get a sad feeling whenever Seneca's works are appraised. They believe that Seneca's ideas are broad, but are based on admonitions. However, this belief is largely unreasonable. Philosophical beliefs require extensive periods of study. Moreover, the progression of philosophical practices has always been on a decline. This stems from the fact that the Roman account of the field is a myopic imitation of a Greek antecedent. The unreasonable opinions that have been formed concerning Seneca's works still haunt, and they have influenced the manner in which students approach Greek and Latin studies. However, students have recently adopted a different approach. Seneca is now perceived as an unnoticed great philosopher whose main concerns were about how human beings are their direct influences in life.

Seneca never wrote as a Stoic who sought to create a new principle from its foundation. Instead, he explored the already available set of principles which he found to be in alignment with his beliefs. To completely reconstruct the philosophical practices of Seneca, one would have to treat them in multiple categories. An inference would have to be drawn from the works of earlier Stoics. Thereafter, a need would exist for comparisons to ascertain the areas in which Seneca projected these works in his personal thoughts. At some points, Seneca's thoughts assist in developing and expatiating a particular

Stoic notion, and at other points, he merely disputes some concepts and stresses the importance of therapy in the practice of any philosophical teaching.

Seneca believed he represented an ideal Stoic and made use of the collective "we" whenever he wanted to describe Stoics, even though his writings do not portray him as an orthodox Stoic. He perceived himself as being an independent rationalist who tried to stand out with his Stoic views establishing that he was no disciple of any philosopher. In his piece On the Private Life, Seneca stated that if anyone wanted him to act as his leaders did, he would not yield to the errands of those people. Rather, he would head in the same direction they were headed. Seneca never saw himself as having a lesser status than the earlier Stoics. Instead, he freely disputed their ideas whenever he found them misleading. Moreover, he never supported the disintegration of non-Stoic ideas from his Stoic practices. He willingly adopted notions from other schools if they were useful for his works. He often noted that he saw diverse philosophical notions like ideas being shared during a meeting and splitting them into different parts to be voted for or against. For instance, Seneca believed Plato's metaphysics was encouraging. As much as he did not show any form of support for "Forms" theory, he posited that one would improve generally should one find time for its studies.

Seneca made good use of comparisons and imagery which were known to have been related to other schools of thought. This can be seen in his Plato-inspired representation of the body is a prison for one's soul. However, making use of such ideas does not mean Seneca was in any way committed to the originating theories.

In 2005, Inwood clarified the concept of independence that Seneca explored. He stressed that even though Seneca received his education through Roman scholars, his pattern of thought was completely in Latin. To elaborate on this, one must compare the approaches of Cicero and Seneca.

Cicero diligently notified his reader of the Greek terminologies he interpreted using Latin. Cicero's thoughts can be understood if one has background knowledge of Greek terms. Seneca never tried to associate his thoughts with Greek philosophy or terminologies. Instead, he thought expressly in Latin and wanted those who generated interest in his works to think along the same patterns as well.

Seneca's interest was with Ethics. He had a vast knowledge of epistemology, Logic, and philosophy of language, but did not waste much energy on these other aspects of Stoicism. Veyne once stated that Seneca's philosophy was not a devalued or undignified one that highlighted the Romans' practical actions. Instead, his philosophical practices were a direct representation of his belief that philosophy was a noble field. This made a major contribution to his focus on the issue of Ethics.

In his works, Seneca ensured there was a person whom he constantly addressed. This persona often appeared to be struck with an inward sickness, while Seneca himself would be the resourceful therapist who would run a diagnosis of his patient's mind.

In justifying notions, Seneca hardly used the traditional step-by-step analysis procedures that philosophers adopted. Seneca decided to put his thoughts in letters because his inquisitions move from one aspect of the individual's experiences to the other, from wide to concise arguments or consultations. This technique helps his readers identify themselves with his philosophical notions. To learn from philosophy, Seneca believed insights should not be absorbed passively. They must be put into action as the reading progresses. This would help readers constantly relate things to themselves and gain the ability to give appropriate consent.

Seneca and other subsequent Stoics are known to have rejected the idea of a perfect and comprehensively wise individual whom ancient Stoics had once given the status of Sage. With this, one should not assume Stoics during Seneca's period were displeased or tried to be more realistic. Rather, it should be noted that Seneca's projection about the need to always progress so as to get to that point of perfection eventually is an integral aspect of his philosophical submissions and practices. In the first place, a Sage, according to the early Stoics, could be a reference point in the development of notions. The ancient Stoics' definition of a wise person is based on to what such a person would consent, as well as the ways in which he or she would react to certain situations. Seneca's philosophical practices dictate that humans are to be brought to a good understanding of the intricacies of Stoicism. With this background, notions – such as a wise person's consent – are not necessarily relevant.

What Seneca tried to do was to let readers peek into several situations that could force them to lose grip of their personal perceptions and subsequently become enslaved by fame and money, as well as the reactions generated from life's difficulties. He strove to teach the ways in which individuals could live above some inherent habits, notwithstanding the high probability that such habits would be exhibited. Out of all Seneca's writings, about three of them were labeled as "consolation." This trio is in the form of letters, but they have been argued to be a transformation from philosophical consultations into Seneca's definition of therapy.

In a letter to his mother, Seneca tried to console her over his exile. He depicted his exile in a metaphoric way and subsequently described how he could afford to be a man with multiple personalities. He stated that any situation in which an individual is alienated from his native environment or forcefully separated from it could be likened to the situation of a political exile.

This implies that the interpretation of Seneca's consolations is dependent on individual situations, as well the person being addressed. It is important to note that during his consolations to his mother and to another woman whose child had died, Seneca apprised the issue of virtue in relation to gender. He constantly relayed to his mother that she had been able to live above the normal faults found in women and that the virtue she possessed was a befitting gift. Therefore, she had to strive to avoid being a victim of the grief that females tended to have. Keeping her virtue also meant she could live above the ideal and still be dependent on nature that is resident in the lives of females.

COSMOPOLITANISM ACCORDING TO SENECA

Seneca explained that it has become harder to choose an ideal life among those of politics, pleasure, and theory. Although this assertion was not a Stoic approach, it had been a conventional dispute that can be traced back to the days of Aristotle, who compared the perception of life by a politician and by a theorist. It can also be seen in the interaction between Plato and Aristotle's ideas concerning what is considered good. Seneca never shared the ideology that a difference should exist between a theoretical and practical life. However, Aristotle's pattern of addressing the issue gave Seneca a way to explain the situations he faced and those he addressed – that is, the choice to either independently pursue a political career or to refrain from it altogether.

Seneca, in his works On Peace of Mind and On Private Life, examined the aforementioned options of choosing between a devoted philosophical life and participating in politics. According to Seneca, choosing any option depends on how the individual balances the situation. One must ask how much he or she can take in or endure before one is forced to refrain. In this sense, philosophy functions in two ways. The need exists for philosophical perceptions that would serve as foundations for one's actions. On the other hand, the need exists to spend quality time to discover that virtue is the only good thing to adopt, and in the process, to rediscover one's inner peace.

Politics and philosophy are two fields in which individuals can assist one another. The distinction between political and theoretical life aided Seneca in outlining his perception of cosmopolitanism in Stoicism. However, opting for either politics or philosophy is not the same thing as opting for either practice or theory. Instead, politics and philosophy are two communities which every human being is a part of simultaneously. The political community is the immediate one, while the philosophical community extends to the whole universe. Striving to build a political career means such an individual wants to be beneficial to other members of the immediate community. Adopting a philosophical life means such an individual has chosen to live and please the entire universe altogether. Seneca stressed that the production of philosophical writings and teachings is a good way to assist those who may or may not be within one's vicinity. A wide range of benefits is attached to the study of philosophy as it helps scholars assist other human beings who belong to the world to which they are connected.

Seneca freely asserted that cosmopolitanism is centered on the notion that acting for the benefit of others is good. However, he failed to realize that the idea of cosmopolitanism brings about the issue of having to endlessly struggle to assist everyone around oneself – a task that is largely not achievable.

In contrast to Seneca's description, cosmopolitanism helps humans be free. It is possible that a philosopher would be in a preferable state to assist others than a political figure such as a Roman senator. Because the two things are perceived as being good, individuals are pleased with the lives they have chosen. A kind of life projected by cosmopolitanism is so helpful that a limited political concept may not contain it. Assisting others should not be carried out only by those who are valued in the localities.

Seneca stated in On the Private Life that the most important action any individual can carry out is to be helpful to other humans. Cosmopolitanism revolves around a perception of human nature; the way human beings are is simply a result of the natural connection that exists among them. The Stoics believe that humans are fragments of a larger whole, and Seneca also had that inclination. In his work On Benefits, a piece that dwelled on "Beneficere" (translated as "doing good") was explained as a social representation. Seneca questioned God's doings being ultimately for the benefit of human beings. He stated that human beings, to a large extent, do not have natural arms when compared to other animals. This means human beings are the weaker ones. Surprisingly, God gave human beings the ability to have supreme control over other animals. Despite the vulnerability of human beings, God gave them an edge over other animals with His provision of cohesion and reason. As soon as human relations are not cohesive, mankind will be thrown into chaos instantly as it is the core of human existence. Seneca's idea of human cohesion aligns with the earlier Stoic notion concerning "oikeiôsis" (the innate connection among humans), as well as the idea that the universe is one gigantic being with human beings as the body parts.

SENECA'S PSYCHOLOGY

A Stoic Description of the Human Soul

Stoicism has two main approaches to the description of the human soul. While the first approach dwells on the idea that human beings have a physical soul of sorts, the other approach explains that a mature human soul is rational, indulges the assistance of reason, and agrees with the idea of oneness. Although Seneca valued Plato's depiction of the soul as being of higher moral standards when compared to things of the human body, he was particularly convinced about the Stoic conception that the human soul is physical. Seneca found explanations of this aspect to be worth studying against the remedial nature of the notions that surround virtue, which he enjoyed. However, in one of his Letters, Seneca explained the importance of equating the human soul with a physical body. This is because bodies are generally responsible for acting on things such as impulses, as well as causes and effects.

Ancient Stoicism is believed to have been divided into three tiers: the early phase, dominated by Zeno, Chrysippus, and others; the middle phase, during which Posidonius thrived; and, of course, the late phase, in which Seneca found himself. This classification represents the different stages of the development of Stoic philosophical psychology as well as the inquisition into the possibility that Posidonius and Panaetius digressed from the psychological concept of oneness. The psychological concept of oneness suggests that no part of the human soul is rational. Instead, the soul, in all ramifications, is rational and united. The concept of oneness dictates that enthusiastic disputes and unreasonable acts are not produced through an altercation between reasonable and unreasonable parts of the human soul. Rather, unreasonable thoughts or acts should be seen as a conditionally unpleasant part of a genuinely reasonable soul.

The concept of oneness in Stoicism is, to a large extent, a contrast to the notion of the human soul as posited by Aristotle and Plato. The psychological concept also had considerable influence on the notion of Ethics, action, and emotion. It remains hard to ascertain whether the middle phase of ancient Stoicism derailed from this psychological concept. For long periods, several reasonable arguments insisted that it actually did.

However, influential studies have in recent times tried to discredit such arguments. Contrary to initial thoughts, the early and middle phases of ancient Stoicism must have aligned in more ways than imagined. Research conducted on the works of Seneca revealed that there is no use trying to understand whether Stoicism in Rome supported either the uniform approach of early Stoicism or the diverse approach adopted in its middle phase.

Seneca must have agreed with the concept of oneness because he never felt a distinction existed between the reasonable and unreasonable capabilities of the human soul. As well, he reformed a similar part of the notion of the human soul as explained by early Stoics. Furthermore, the psychological concept of oneness means reason has no theoretical or practical differences. Action is a direct product of knowledge. No doubt, all forms of knowledge in philosophy help make good decisions. According to Hadot, this means no cogent difference exists in developing notions and trying to have a good life.

Seneca approached the idea from a personal perspective. He believed the decision to study arguments for only a specific reason does not guarantee peace. In one of his Letters, Seneca clearly emphasized that he personally did not derive pleasure from the creation of valid arguments for a set of ideas which were merely penned in notes. He stressed that only the practice of virtue could usher in happiness. One of those he addressed, Lucilius, was pictured as having encouraged him to state every supporting or opposing notion important to the aforementioned contentions, and his Letter 85 tried to yield to the encouragement by addressing some of the points that had been raised. However, as vividly depicted in all Seneca's pieces, such propositions are not adequate, nor are they ideally fitting. Instead, the relevance of Stoic propositions should be thought of and processed in different aspects of their practical representations. That way, one would understand the ways to follow their dictates. An instance is when an individual either has or has not been voted into a position; such an individual would either be richer than – or not as rich as – others, respectively. It is expected that individuals align their thoughts with this analysis because a careful consideration of such would ultimately reflect in the patterns their lives take.

At this juncture, an important question to ask is whether the support of practical philosophy is not a direct contrast to Stoicism's notion of reason. This practical approach may mean that if humans grasp any idea whatsoever, such an idea has turned into a branch of knowledge which would subsequently control human actions. However, Seneca opined that a big difference exists between having precise knowledge of an idea and conceiving that such ideas are right and influential in the personal lives of individuals. He then proceeded to cite an instance: even though he believed traveling in either an extravagant or lowly carriage does not make a difference, he felt a bit embarrassed whenever he was making use of a lowly one. The questions, then, are: Why should he have felt that way? Why would Seneca have given consent to Plato's notion that the wishes of humans for popularity and wealth would eventually project their pride as long as such tendencies had not been suppressed? Should there be a reason why the supposed comprehensive structure of philosophy and the detailed research on contrasting ideologies are not necessarily important in living a good life?

With his position, Seneca appeared to have reduced the standard of the older Stoic description of knowledge and virtue. In regards to the personal opinions of various scholars, it could be assumed that Seneca merely tried to offer solutions to the rigidity associated with the older descriptions.

The Human Personality and Willingness

A Stoic depiction of the human mind or soul has an extensive inclusion of important notions whose roots are found in epistemology. All human souls have been imprinted with one opinion or another and an individual gets his or her ideas by giving consent to the opinion. As mentioned earlier, at all points humans can give consent to any opinion, oppose it or refuse to reach any conclusion about it. As humans possess this ability, we are responsible for being wise by consenting consciously to reasonable opinions that depict situations in their exact structure. Furthermore, actions are drawn from consenting to practicable opinions, while these consents trigger strong desires or wishes. As long as there is no constraint, the strong desires result in actions. Human beings are solely responsible for exhibiting virtue as giving consent is within one's capability. Individual actions are a result of personal decisions. Seneca tried to analyze these processes using the term "Voluntas," a word completely abstract to Greek Stoicism.

Seneca was assumed to have either been the proponent of will or the one who laid its foundations. It is hard to adequately ascertain the processes that led to the development of "will." Apparently, Velle (wants) and Voluntas (willingness) were dominantly employed in quite a number of arguments projected by Seneca. The question is: Did Seneca believe there was a different division for will that assists the concept of oneness? Could it be said that he had the passion for delving into the phenomenon of personal development and the process of making decisions, prompting him to explain some psychological practices as processes of Velle (willingness)? The latter proposition appears to be plausible and encapsulates a huge portion of the relevant aspects of the original description. This is also because Seneca continued emphasizing why humans must constantly be determined to improve themselves. Seneca's interpretation of psychological practices, called "assent" by older Stoics, is probably more valuable (not having anything to do with a replacement in the components of the notion). This could partially be a result of Seneca's constant use of expressions that are metaphoric in nature.

In place of adopting the general explanation that through the decision-making process humans consent to a practicable opinion, Seneca projected humans as determinants who preside over all the things in which they are expected to be involved, as well as giving compulsory instructions to one another.

In the emotional aspects, Seneca created a distinction between uncontrollable responses (referred to as proto-emotions by older Stoics) and completely developed ones which constitute consent making them controllable. They are considered controllable because the ability to give consent resides within the individual involved. This explanation is an important principle in Stoicism, as it implies that whether one is bright or dumb, everyone has the capability to either give consent or not. In other instances, Seneca used the standard idea of willingness. He explained that actions that showcase virtue are those that can only be considered as reasonable. Others are generated from unreasonable progressions in the human mind, like an emotion. This also means voluntary actions are those that can be seen as virtuous.

Furthermore, Seneca's explanation of self-development poses another challenge. The question is: Did Seneca create the "self?" In one of Seneca's pieces, On Anger, an extract narrates how Seneca explained the ways in which he would personally assess himself every evening. It forced him to ask whether a probe into his insistence constitutes a retrace to his "self" as it had appeared to a number of enthusiasts who had been motivated by the manner in which Foucault explained the process. Could it be said that Seneca was interested in the act of molding oneself?

To process the thought about whether he created or produced the "self," one must differentiate its multiple forms. The foremost step is to inquire whether Seneca developed the psychological concept of oneness to give way to an inward check of the idea (through a pattern that causes the "self" to assume a difficult position which Greek Stoics could not have envisioned for the reasonable human soul). In a second way, one may want to believe that the reason readers of Foucault's propositions have assumed that Seneca's thoughts are modern may be because Seneca was particularly interested in the personal structuring of an individual's life. The latter approach is not as strong as the former, and it has received wider acceptance. Inwood has strongly criticized the initial approach.

Although Seneca has asked that human beings constantly reflect on their personal lives, it should not be considered an attempt to reform the traditional Stoic notions of human souls. Another question might be asked: Would it be acceptable to misuse Seneca's concepts for individual functions having it at the back of one's mind that one is attempting a particular form of involvement with the "self," which has a lot more in common with the present times than with a specific explanation of his contributions?

Veyne had this to say: *"Stoicism has thus become, for our use, a philosophy of the active turning in on itself. It was nothing of the kind in its own day, but the Letters permit us to view it as such."*

Seneca's explanation of the ways in which humans should adopt the idea that virtuous living is the only good way to develop oneself might appear to indicate that he held worldly competitiveness and extravagant modes of living responsible for making such a practice an uneasy one. Seneca emphasized that humans are the ones responsible for their challenges. He indicated to his readers that by standing in each other's ways, they cause their actions to draw them backward or to morph into unpleasant issues. Due to this notion of constant reflection on personal thoughts, Hadot propounded what is known as "spiritual exercises" from the phase of Stoicism.

Taking care of one's soul encompassed Socrates' concept of striving to understand oneself. In Natural Questions, Seneca expressed that a provision of mirrors had been made by nature so that humans can personally understand themselves.

This mode of reaching one's inner self, as Seneca prescribed, has on many occasions not been virtuously deployed. For instance, youths recognize the strength they possess, and that brings them to understand that it is the period of enlightenment and fearlessness. However, understanding oneself is hugely dependent upon philosophical considerations as well as personal reflections.

Again, Seneca stated that public and private lifestyles complement one another. This blend might indicate that the practice of developing the structure of one's soul may, in the end, constitute what has been referred to by the Stoics as "affiliation." Stoic notion dictates that human beings should be appreciative of the fact that all things on the exterior of the mind belong to them. This involves the physical body, other human beings, some other geographical environments in the world, and the universe in its entirety. This implies that as human beings try to establish a middle ground between exclusive philosophical lifestyles and political lifestyles. We are all working toward being good parts of our immediate environment – and, by extension, the entire universe.

Like St. Augustine, a philosopher whose related notion of the inward turn to oneself has constantly been argued for and against, Seneca believed an inward turn to the soul is not sufficient – hence, the need to approach God. Seneca distinctly stated that the turn toward God and nature is influenced by the importance of taking care of the soul and not because of a particular affection for God. Seneca opined, in Natural Questions, that constant reflections within the human soul are merely a preparatory procedure. After successfully living above the aggressive emotions and destabilizations of an outward lifestyle, one may not have been able to be free completely from oneself. In other words, one is not totally free from extreme worry over one's specific needs and wants. This means individuals must reach inwardly into themselves, and also deny themselves. From the concerns of oneself which border questions of Ethics, one must face studying theology as well as nature.

In what ways would this set human beings free? It elevates one from immediate worries and creates a provision of a detailed, distinctive angle concerning them. The research on nature is conducted in a bid to live beyond mortal shortcomings. Beyond that, the concept of virtue, which is at the center of caring for one's mind or soul, is also a concept of having the same qualifications as God. This idea is probably strange to recent psychological therapy approaches as well as to Foucault's notion of caring for oneself.

The Emotional Therapy

Contemplations similar to the Stoic concept of oneness have, on most occasions, been explained with reference to the emotions theory. Importance is attached to whether human beings believe that unreasonable passions or wishes may override good reasoning or are just the unreasonable activities of a rather reasonable mind. Seneca's approach to emotions has been comprehensively examined for traces of the two aforementioned views. Sorabji expressed that Seneca had positioned his notions of the emotions in relation to the early and middle phases of Stoic principles, which are different from his.

Fillon Lahille approached Seneca's On Anger with critical techniques. Others ultimately opined that On Anger could be approached as a concise piece of writing on emotions, one that naturally aligns with the Stoic conception of psychological oneness due to the comprehensive approach that Seneca employed toward it, especially on aggressive emotions.

The Stoics believe that a perfect personality does not exhibit any form of emotion. The Stoic notion of emotions is not focused on reasonable limits or sufficient reactions to emotions. Instead, the focus is on a life devoid of emotions. However, the Stoic did not state that an ideal personality is particularly unmovable. Reasonable responses and tendencies substitute for emotions. The perfect personality has an upright feeling of having a wish (substitute for desire), happiness (substitute for pleasure), and vigilance (substitute for fear). A perfect personality possesses proto-emotions, which implies natural psychological and emotional responses and not a result of consent.

The ideology of reasonable or good emotions – the emotional tendencies and responses of a wise individual as well as proto-emotion – make Stoic presuppositions on the emotions not as impracticable as they are occasionally regarded. Yet, those who study old ideologies of emotions would have perceived that it was right to support the Aristotelian approach, which has the idea that there are sufficient quantifiable emotions.

For instance, when an individual perpetrates a criminal act, is it not right to be furious? Seneca also questioned whether a perfect individual would not be filled with anger if he or she witnessed the rape or mutilation of his or her parents. He explained that it is normal to respond. However, one's reaction should not reflect excessive emotions or actions, like a prompt attack, irrespective of the effectiveness of such responses. Seneca posited that the notion of "moderate emotion" is as unreasonable as the notion of "moderate madness." Human emotions are basically unreasonable, and it is impossible for an unreasonable act to be controlled, specifically because it is unreasonable. Therefore, it is not possible to have appropriate emotions. Rather, they should be replaced with reasonable reactions. A perfect personality would come to the defense of others through the notion of duty, but not with a mind already dominated with desires for vengeance or fury.

Seneca's comprehensive explanation of anger supplements the understanding of the specific ways in which Stoics prescribed the idea that emotions are results of acquired beliefs.

Ancient Stoics outlined that emotions can be classified into four generic classes. These are pleasure (being satisfied concerning a thing), pain (being distraught or uneasy), fear, and desire. Pleasure is expressed as an assumed conditional good, while pain is assumed to be a conditionally bad state. Desire is expressed as a good futuristic occurrence, while fear is expressed as a bad futuristic experience.

Because emotions are strong wishes, they usually end up being acted upon as long as no form of external restriction exists. Anger can be said to be a form of desire. When angry, the individual gives consent to the opinion that he or she should embark upon reciprocation. The original decision that prompts anger can be a statement such as "He hurt me." On Anger aided in explaining the patterns in which multiple decisions can be represented within a single emotion, as well as the ways in which emotion has been linked to unreasonable acts.

Other aspects upon which Seneca dwelled extensively were grief and fear, as well as those emotions with tendencies to control individuals' lives because of the mortal nature of human beings. The fear associated with death is contradictory in the sense that it strives to keep life, but it simultaneously destroys it. It is necessary to accept the inevitability of death. Fear causes humans to lose control of their minds, erasing one's reasoning faculty. One cannot completely live above grief or fear if one has yet to renew one's perception about death's preconceived bad nature. Death should be perceived as a natural phenomenon. Awareness of this fact is partly knowledge of nature itself. Human beings are frightened of the things about which they have inadequate knowledge. Therefore, fear is cured through knowledge.

Seneca emphasized two processes of death. He explained that death could mean a movement into the life beyond, or it could be a real termination of the body and soul. Seneca dwelled more on some confusing situations in his tragedies. The tragedies may depict unreasonable reactions to death, or they could be proof of the notion that compassionate philosophical doctrines are not enough to relegate these deep thoughts or imaginations.

Seneca asked intriguing questions in an excerpt from On Peace of Mind: Why the perceived perfect personality wouldn't act immorally, as well as why such a person would not have a bad feeling concerning it? This sort of question relates to an important part of the Stoic ideology. Although four forms of emotions have been stipulated, there are only three forms of reasonable feelings. They are desire, fear, and pleasure. Pain has no reasonable correlation with the emotions one has presumed to be bad. A wise individual would not conclude that a lack of wealth or sickness is not a good thing. Such a person would understand that the only bad is immorality. The question is, why did such an individual not categorically make the conclusion or decision that immorality is not good in a manner such that emotional positions of "reasonable bad thoughts" align with it?

In this view, Seneca responded that virtue gains in the alliance with a traditional Stoic proposition. A Sage would always wear a happy look instead of being weighed down by sadness. This is because the individual's positivity creates possibilities. As concise as Seneca's response may seem, it comprehensively covered the most important aspect of the debate that influences the Stoic position on "negative moral feelings." It may be because virtue does not permit reasonable negative emotion-based reactions because such reactions would not be beneficial.

CLEMENCY

In Seneca's explanation of the ways in which a virtuous individual reacts to the flaws in other individuals, he elaborated on the Stoic range of opinions on reasonable emotions to encompass clementia. Seneca's piece, On Mercy, has constantly proven difficult to understand fully, even for historians. He compliments the good acts of a young Nero, which contrast with his unkind acts, difficulty, and sympathy, Seneca seemed to have laid the foundation for a form of literature called "mirrors for princes." Whether Seneca decided to snub it or was not aware of Nero's crimes at the time cannot be ascertained. The best interpretation is that he was able to relate to Nero's reasons for doing so later.

There is a challenge in translating the Latin clementia into an appropriate English word. While some refer to it as mercy, others choose to describe it as clemency. This means Seneca tried to bring an uncommon virtue to prominence. In On Mercy, Seneca addressed clementia as a superior virtue – a sort of elevation that was equally new to Stoic Ethics. Older Stoics never postulated that virtues had to fit into some specific roles or functions. Rather, they preached that the possession of virtue would ultimately make such persons stand out in whatever role they found themselves. Seneca's idea of clemency is known to have originated from a sort of self-description used by the Romans. Clemency was originally a virtue that Rome practiced with whichever city or whomever they had conquered. This means clemency was once a gesture shown toward Rome's enemies. It was not a virtue that natural Romans practiced. During Caesar's reign, clementia was transformed into a virtue that could only be possessed by an emperor.

According to Seneca, clemency is a sort of controlled behavior which an individual who possesses power adopts in place of being harsh or hitting whoever must have offended him or her. It is also related to the practice of equity. To an extent, the foremost practice of clementia cannot be considered a virtue in Stoicism. This is because a virtuous individual is not expected to exhibit cruel behavior that must be contained through clementia.

EQUITY

There is also a contention as to whether the practice of equity – a leader's power to carry out judgments with the help of different presented variables and not through laid-down rules – is fitting with Stoic philosophy. In Greek, equity means epieikeia, a notion explained in Aristotle's Nicomachean ethical dictates. In it, he explained a popular issue by mentioning that the law is a general stipulation. However, individual situations must be addressed within their contexts. The equity virtue is a justice-seeking one. In this sense, it tries to find modifications to a rather fixed and rigid set of rules. Although some doxography texts expressed the notion that the Stoics don't believe equity is a characteristic of a wise individual, the passages are assumed to have been pointing out the fact that the Stoics never shared Aristotle's idea of equity – a practice that sought to offer solutions to a supposed lapse or lapses in common laws, as an attitude of a wise individual. The Stoics' conception of law is not as it is stipulated in a political setting. Rather, what could be considered an ideal law is that which is similar to reason – that is, the activity that must be carried out. In Stoic terms, equity is perceived as the ability to make judgments about situations after careful consideration of all the scenarios involved. Addressing equity from this angle makes it agree with the general notion of Ethics in Stoicism.

VIRTUE – SUITABLE AND RIGHT ACTION

The differences between good and valuable things, as outlined in Stoicism, are central to the Letters written by Seneca. Although value is inherent in wealth and health, the preferred indifferents virtue remains the only good there is. In multiple instances, Seneca explained the ways in which wealth and health do not determine genuine happiness. His views did not approach the notion by enlisting strict directives like they had to be compulsorily acted on. He addressed his reader directly with instances as understandable in his time as they are now. Human beings have the tendency to believe that traveling without any expense would make the world a better place. However, human beings become discouraged when, for instance, one must settle for less than fresh bread.

In addressing these comprehensive conditions, Seneca continued to emphasize the most important idea of Ethics in Stoicism. This is the fact that only virtue can yield genuine happiness and this is without any contribution by other factors. The so-called preferred indifferents are actually valuable, even though they cannot be seen as "good" according to Stoic ideology. Scholars later opined that Seneca believed wealth and health are worthless altogether and that a need existed to preach constantly against them. Scholars cited the comparisons and instances that Seneca employed. Seneca wrote that having a detailed understanding of how hard it was not to perceive entities like wealth and health as good things are what determined human happiness. In the same vein, he continued citing clear instances in a bid to help his reader have less flair for other things that seemed valuable to him or her (he never directly posited that such things as wealth and health must be seen as unimportant or not properly cared for).

A similar and valuable area of Ethics in Stoicism is the contrast between suitable and right action. Suitable actions consider indifferents. Wise and foolish persons are capable of acting suitably. However, only a wise individual would act ideally suitable or in the right manner. A wise person's actions are reflections of his or her corresponding thoughts and showcase the regularity of his or her mind. Seneca's explanations follow this pattern. He emphasized that it is important to consider all indifferents – preferred or not – as being valuable or not. However, goodness is not achieved in acquiring or retrieving them.

Responding to the meaning of virtue, Seneca stressed that virtue implies a judgment that showcases strict truth. Seneca argued that placing any form of importance on the indifferents can be compared to a situation in which a better haircut is used to judge two good individuals. This sort of inference was necessary to ensure that Seneca adequately described, in figurative ways, the position of the value in indifferents. One is drawn to the fact that a good haircut is not a relevant metric. Seneca did not perceive it that way. In comparison to goodness, indifferents labeled as "preferred" are as unimportant as a nice haircut when they are placed side by side with virtue, even though they can be seen as possessing value. This means the preferred indifferents can be compared only to those which are preferred, not as having the same status as the good.

In suitable action, the individual recognizes things with inherent value. However, this process does not simply occur. Such an individual does not generally make comparisons between the value of health and wealth; instead, he or she figures out the manner through which a particular event and the available actions within it relate to indifferents (for instance, the process of dressing up to suit a specific occasion). Because the situation in which an individual act is relevant to suitable action, the Stoics obviously created some extensive writings through which they projected the ways in which such constituents affect the things one is expected to do. Letters 94 and 95 by Seneca appear to be instances of extensive writings. As it remains a fact that those pieces were written, adequate proof exists that indifferents are not merely unimportant, but subjects to contemplate. For some time, Seneca's Letters 94 and 95 were studied with an intention to ascertain whether rules apply to Ethics in Stoicism.

This inquisition is important to the explanation of the Stoic ideology of the law. For a long time, the Stoics had been seen as the ancient proponents of natural constitutions. Because the Stoics came up with tenet-like prescriptions, this can imply that the Stoics saw the law as constituting tenets.

In the two aforementioned Letters, Seneca explained two ideas. The first is praecepta, and the other one is called decreta. These two terms can be translated as "precepts" and "principles," respectively. Seneca's explanation was centered on the question if one seeks a good existence by delving into philosophical studies, is there a need to study just decreta (principles), or is there a need to also study praecepta? In line with the initial stance, to obtain virtue, one must dedicate oneself to the central rules of Stoicism. This is what Seneca called decretal, and this means decreta cannot be said to be practicable guides or basic ideas. Rather, they can be seen as very abstract ideas of philosophy which were fundamentally taught by the Stoics.

The other stance that Seneca appeared to support stipulates that the study of only the original set of guides in Stoicism is not adequate. The need also exists to reflect deeply on the requirements and the importance of studying praecepta is similar to the original set of guides or principles. This may imply that this sort of approach encompasses some instructions. In this scenario, one is expected to act in this manner. It remains uncertain that Seneca distinctly set such instructions. Nonetheless, everyone who seeks to understand virtue would gain from patterning his or her thoughts on the different situations that may come one's way deliberating on the ways in which the components of each situation are important to suitable actions. This ultimately develops a greater knowledge of the worth of those things that are valuable (or not) to humans. Seneca's examples – for instance, a woman who married early should not receive the same treatment that another who has yet to be married receives – probably sharpen students' knowledge of the sorts of problems that are important to suitable action.

Furthermore, Seneca projected a counselor who constantly makes humans think about ideas, like happiness not being a product of wealth. However, this sort of expression does not seem to be a guideline or instruction. In conclusion, the counselor is an individual who can fashion a suggestion for a corresponding situation. In Letter 71, Seneca also stressed that suggestions are fine-tuned to specific occasions and take different forms as the occasion changes. When an individual requires advice, such an individual does not seek to be filled in with the appropriate instructions so as to neutralize the situation. Rather, such a person seeks ways to weigh deliberations.

BEING OF BENEFIT TO OTHER HUMANS

Regarding the notion of the good, the Stoics are perceived as being very vocal with their statement that virtue is the only good. They also equated the good with "benefit." Seneca, too, adopted this ancient idea that benefits are resident in the good. As has been revealed, Seneca believed political and philosophical lives are good patterns of living when done appropriately, specifically because the two patterns of living are beneficial to others. In addressing the benefits life in line with philosophy gives unto others, Seneca stated that an individual whose life exemplifies virtue has benefits he or she already gives, even without being involved in any political action whatsoever. The way such a person walks, his or her underlying consistency, and facial expressions are beneficial. In the same vein that some forms of medicines are instantly effective through their smells, the good effects of virtue can be perceived even without physical proximity to others. Seneca used a whole comprehensive piece to treat the way in which humans should be of benefit to others, as well as the way humans should treat the reception of benefits.

On Benefits remains the lengthiest of the old pieces that Seneca wrote on a specific topic relating to Ethics. The piece of writing is grounded within a social context in Rome. Its comprehensive descriptions and copious examples give it a status higher than that of a historical document. Seneca addressed good acts as well as unnecessary favors, polite and impolite forms of receptions, the happiness derived, or difficulty experienced in returning a favor, and, finally, appreciation and covetousness. Seneca's subject is the two-phase version of a sort anthropological discussion such as an exchange of gifts, the precise structure of the topics discussed back then in Rome and the ideas to support the fact that it is only an individual who possesses the good that can benefit others. This contrast created a rather complex piece. It is little wonder that useful literature was scarcely available. However, this condition had been improved through recent interpretations which involve philosophical additions by Miriam Griffin, John Cooper, et al.

What could be the definition of benefits as Seneca used the term? Benefits can be any sort of assistance an individual may render to another who may also belong to a group so that the unity of the group is made stronger creating socialization in the process. Some instances are: rendering assistance, such as giving out money or material things; using one's position to help another individual or a member of such a person's family; helping foster another human's safety or well-being; protecting another human being from destruction or serious damages; standing in for another individual; helping advance another person's career; instructing and providing education when capable; guiding and giving advice to others and so on.

Generally, benefits are exchanged among humans who are not from related families. They are not the same as the duties expected to be performed by a child or wife, or the responsibilities of an employee or servant. The things parents do for their wards are considered benefits and cannot be called mere duties. Children, when they help their parents, are only giving back what they owe, thereby actualizing the activities related to their duties. Seneca declared that children could be of benefit to their parents. For instance, if children cause their parents to receive positive remarks through groundbreaking milestones, such things are invaluable gifts. In Book 3, Seneca discussed the idea that servants can be beneficial to those whom they serve once they have carried out more activities than those they were originally designated to do. Seneca believed that because compulsion could be annoying to anyone, servants' beneficial acts showcase a fascinating capability to live above the fury of having such statuses as theirs.

In addition, when an individual lends money, he or she has not provided any form of benefit. Money should be given for free whenever one claims to be rendering a favor. Truly, if an individual doesn't want to be part of the form of socialization that the exchange of benefits elicits, such an individual should only receive money like he had been loaned.

For instance, when an individual one never wanted in one's affairs becomes responsible for one's freedom from jail because such a person had paid the bail, one may accept the offer. However, it is expected that such monies would be returned as soon as one can do so. In that manner, no connection would have been created. The contrast between permanent and temporary giving was discussed at every point in Seneca's piece, and it led to two further views.

The first view dictates that the appropriate habits of giving out, accepting, and giving back benefits entail freedom. The character being addressed in On Benefits was named Liberalis. Before a thing can be considered a benefit, it should not have been given out reluctantly with a grudge or at an annoyingly slow pace. A supposed good act should not become burdensome to the receiver if such a deed is to have the status of being accepted rightly and willingly. The sort of feeling that showcases the right habits on all sides is the feeling of happiness. All other things would suggest reluctance, worries about unwanted connections, and others. Second, the contrast between giving out and lending can be likened to the contrast between fairness and good acts. Seneca perceived justice as less important because adopting it would mean that trust or confidence is placed on rigid rules instead of human souls. If the area of "good acts" is dominated by habits in accordance with legal agreements, Seneca opined that a very valuable thing would go missing.

All through the extensive writing, Seneca emphasized habits and not fact-based actions. Returning a favor or transferring some objects do not matter. A giver's corresponding state of mind is where genuine favor resides. In the same vein, the appreciative state of the receiver's mind determines genuine favor reception. The willingness to provide benefits, as well as the willingness to return such favors, are the necessary acts for appropriate giving and receiving.

Some other scholars have opined that actions can be considered right only because of an act of willingness. These assertions are central to the tenets of Ethics in Stoicism. Scholars perceive Seneca's Book 4 as a portion of his formal writings to explain additional abstract thoughts aimed at infusing an explanation of the historic traditional activities in Rome with the ethical rules in Stoicism.

The examination can be said to have been a process of comparative deduction. Book 4 has more explanations and detailed propositions of Stoicism than other pieces. Seneca explained God's given benefits by the Stoic perception of nature and the notion of theology. Seneca's inquisition into whether benefits should be given due to what they constitute or based on a personal advantage the giver receives is not in any way a typical Stoic belief. In fact, it contrasts with the core structure of ethical tenets in earlier Stoic practices. The Stoics believe that advantages and the good are not different in disposition.

However, as expected, Seneca's Book 4 does not explain the subtlety of the notion of good in Stoicism due to a tendency toward theorizing such discussions. His propositions concerning good acts are recorded concisely in Books 1-3. The assertion that what matters are intention and attitude had already been grounded in manners which are relatively free from the Stoic propositions concerning the good. This was done through the statement about the differences between responsibilities and benefits. It explains the consequences of making others worry over tasks to which they would not eventually measure up, and that there must be a way to return favors even when they do not have the material luxury to do so. Seneca explained the constraints that would probably arise within a community that constantly practices giving and returning favors. In a situation in which inadequate giving exists, the receivers ideally lose their independence and ultimately develop the feeling of being at the mercy of their givers.

Many parts of Seneca's On Benefits exhibit standards which seek to stipulate the ways to go about giving, accepting from others, and returning benefits. However, his propositions relied on what he called the truth about the psychological nature of human beings. For instance, he believed that the unpleasant parts of the way human beings act toward others tend to be stuck in the recipients' minds for longer periods than the pleasant ones. Human beings have the natural tendency to develop new passions, which makes it difficult to remember the benefits received in the past. What human beings process instead are their current and future needs and aspirations. Appropriate giving includes identifying these stated truths. Seneca stated that human beings are digressive and come to other's assistance only with a grudge. It is little wonder that an individual's unwillingness to express his or her thoughts becomes more objectified in others' minds. It is also little wonder that no form of respect is given to such forms of unkind giving.

If there is an assumption that Seneca was correct about the idea that it is hard to be good at assisting, the attention of an ethical description of assistance should not be based on the measure or level of assistance that should be given. Instead, it should be based on the ways in which one achieves a complex or not-so-common feat – that is, to assist in a way in which the receiver would not ultimately become more miserable due to the assistance. Among all pieces on moral ideologies in the modern world, the only piece that has similarity to Seneca's On Benefits is Doctrine of Virtue by Kant. It is a piece that constitutes the acclaimed "casuistical" aspects in which Kant explained issues such as the ways in which some forms of assistance would reduce the personal esteem of the receiver, as well as others' perceptions of such persons, thereby rendering the recipients as inferiors and having statuses beneath the givers.

Even though their foundational reasons are not similar, Seneca and Kant agree on the following point. A morally right giving might even mean that the receiver would not be aware of it. This is to avoid unpleasant outcomes. The classification of being a receiver and, by extension, a dependent can become more prominent than the act of being beneficial. Seneca's approach revealed that he supported common reasoning which states that the inability to express gratitude is a very bad shortcoming. Still, he believed that incorrect giving comes before and is always the result of bad reception or an inability to pay back. Seneca's Book 1 and Book 2 dwelled extensively on this notion.

DOING GOOD

In his 120th Letter, Seneca discussed how the ideology of the good is formulated. This process is a dominant area of inquisition in ethical studies in Stoicism. The Stoics assume that, through the growing process, humans learn to be rational, which involves learning prolepseis (preconception). As soon as an individual possesses a small amount of reasoning ability, he or she would become developed and begin to approach the perfection stage of his or her rational ability. At a stage of such an individual's progress, he or she would then learn and imbibe the ideology of the good. The process is one in which a human eventually and comprehensively understands that virtue is the only good there is. At that stage, the ideology of a foolish individual would have been transformed into a wise one. The individual would have a scientific notion of the good. He or she would have completely learned the notion of the good that does things correctly. Once this notion has been acquired, one cannot easily be deceived by such notions as "happiness comes only from wealth." Isn't it obvious that human beings have a preconceived notion of the good before ultimately becoming wise individuals when they do?

The need exists to identify two distinct concepts. The first is that human beings already have an innate conception of the good. Everyone labels some things as good even before he or she have any comprehensive knowledge of the facts of Stoicism. The second concept is that the progressive nature of human beings can drive them to realize and relate with the Stoic notion that practicing virtue is the only form of good humans can exhibit, even without having the adequate ability to give credit to its reality in their lives constantly. This progressiveness is what Seneca tried to pass on in almost all his writing. His 120th Letter appeared to have added to the

Stoic notion of the achievement of the ideology of the good exactly in this manner.

Seneca, in contrast to Cicero, did not explain the progressive stages through which an individual becomes a wise person. Instead, he explained how humans gain knowledge of the things to which the Stoic refers whenever they posit that virtue is the only good (in an instance in which no one, including oneself, is living virtuously). When one studies noble acts, one instantly augments the virtuous characteristics of the actors but reduces the proclamation of their unpleasant acts. Through these processes and other related mental tasks, one ultimately understands the ideal structure of virtue. This understanding prompts one to perceive the goodness in virtue without necessarily having a typical experience of virtue. The Stoics believed an encounter with a perfectly wise individual is rare and hard to come by.

THEOLOGY AND PHYSICS: PRACTICING NATURAL PHILOSOPHY

In Natural Questions, Seneca wrote extensive pieces that discussed meteorology. However, modern readers are not so enthusiastic when they examine Natural Questions. To be fair, what is there to examine in elaborate explanations of lights, rain, the clouds, wind, earthquakes, thunder, and the comprehensive analysis of rivers such as the Nile? Another puzzle to unravel is why Seneca spent a lot of time on these occurrences. Students appraise Seneca's Natural Questions in contrast to the idea behind basic meteorology, which has existed for a long time.

According to Graver (2000), Seneca was arguably involved in a task that was properly established. The distinct additions to meteorology all have similar submissions. The reasonable description of any natural occurrence is believed to have the ability to change how humans live their lives in general. For instance, an individual who has knowledge of the causes and operations of lightning and thunder would not have a misconception that it is Zeus' way of informing him or her about his anger. Graver explained that at the age when Seneca wrote Natural Questions, such forms of controversies were common among the Epicureans. Physics in Epicureanism is known to have dwelled strongly on how to combat fear and superstitious beliefs. It is assumed that anyone who believes Zeus communicates with him or her is grossly confused. However, those who are knowledgeable about the ways in which these natural elements are structured could live rationally and ideally.

A Stoic who seeks to write about these phenomena would be constrained in some ways. The Epicurean philosophy dictates that God never bothers himself with the structure or patterns of human lives to the extent that he would warn against certain forms of activities by expressing his dissatisfaction.

In contrast, Stoics perceive God to be loving, kind and bothered about the occurrences in human lives. Therefore, the skepticism constantly situated within meteorological occurrences must be combated with comprehensive, realistic, and physical explanations. The position that God is not moved to provide warnings is not available in this scenario. Rather, Seneca supported the idea that God would have ways of warning human beings, and that is why divination can be seen as a form of science.

In all, the notion behind Natural Questions is to weigh God's value, to examine the universe as a whole, to give credit to Godly acts and activities, and to liberate human beings from fears invoked by some natural occurrences. Being knowledgeable about thunder and the clouds are fascinating because human beings aspire to grasp how these phenomena are formulated. More importantly, it must add to one's general development and aid in actualizing excellence.

Seneca strove to find the solution to the persistent fear that had been evoked by natural occurrences, thereby apprising meteorology through an ethical angle. Natural Questions consists of some explanations of individuals who are fond of behaviors that Seneca perceived as unpleasant and morally bad. The excerpts are generally known to be evasive. Williams (2012) classified Natural Questions as being a step ahead of meteorological practices strictly because the piece is dramatic, full of imagination, and comprehensive. Williams stated that Seneca's writing is creative interaction with nature. Seneca sought to project some of his opinions comparing the fascinating architecture of nature against the unpleasant appearance of evil actions.

Seneca's appraisal of nature is particularly centered on an individual's position and role in the universe. He emphasized that it is ridiculous not to strive to conduct findings on nature as human beings because the human race is a huge part of it. Seneca's cosmopolitan approach is pivotal to the manner in which he led his students into the appraisal of nature. He opined that until human beings see their normal lives from an angle such that they can be equal to the stars, they will never come to understand that wealth, boundaries, and so on are unimportant.

Pierre Hadot referred to this angle as the "view from above" – a perception that frees human beings as long as they are able to view some valuable issues as being trivial. The need exists to study nature so as to gain knowledge of one's daily worries and ultimately be liberated from irrational worries over them.

One could conduct research on nature with the knowledge that one is an aspect of it. In line with his support of the early Stoic notion that the universe is one huge being with bodies and components, Seneca believed humans have the inherent motivation to venture into the study of nature. Therefore, it is important to consistently engage in natural philosophy and dedicate one's life to it.

Seneca distinguished the study of history from that of nature. According to him, it is the aspect of Physics that appears to be not so practical that is actually more practicable. He opined that it was more appropriate to worship the gods than to worship the military expeditions of warriors such as Alexander. The appraisal of nature has value because it is an inquisition about the things that ought to happen as opposed to an inquisition about the events that actually occurred.

NATURAL LAW

The ancient Stoics were seen as the original proponents of the natural law principle. The normal term for such laws in ancient Stoic practices is "common" instead of "natural," as it is being named. Seneca classified rules as being natural and comprehensively explained the laws of nature. The old Stoic perception concerning the law is, in a way, grounded in the concept of correct actions and in another, a realistic narration of the way reason spreads throughout the universe.

The realistic ideology of the law is dominant in Seneca's approach. When examining earthquakes and fears that human beings experience, Seneca highlighted that human beings commit blunders as soon as they begin thinking that there is no danger of natural disasters in some areas. Every area is bound by similar laws. Seneca also highlighted another approach in which he stated that the natural laws control activities under the earth as much as they control what transpires above it. The universe is structured in a way that all the things bound to occur, as well as the worldwide conflagration that has been predicted to be responsible for bringing the world to an end, have been parts of the world since its inception.

Natural occurrences such as earthquakes are helping nature go through its normal processes and design. Because all things to happen were decided at the onset, all things come easily. The appreciation of nature is targeted toward agreeing with the theories of nature, the first of which is the truth that human beings are not immortal. Seneca talked about the inevitability of death as a basic rule of nature. He expressed the notion that death has been agreed upon since one's birth. Science is responsible for proposing the reasons one should not be afraid of death. It is also responsible for projecting the notion that living a philosophical life is of utmost importance, as it exposes human beings to the ability to be ready when death comes. It should enlighten human beings that those forms of death dreaded the most are not so different from other forms of death. The law of nature stipulates that freedom comes from the ability to accept and be ready for death at any point in time. The fact that everyone has equal status at death reveals the fairness of nature.

A discussion that is also available in Seneca's practice of therapy, as well as in his philosophical stance on nature, is "time." The third book in Natural Questions, which is titled "On the Waters of the Earth," starts with explanations about the amount of time the project of natural philosophy requires. It also dwelled on the time he felt had been consumed by worrying over worldly things and, ultimately, the idea that one can retrieve lost time by being diligent with the time presently available. The truth that no one has an infinite life has been stated right from the introductory lines of the piece. Seneca then examined the similarity between the world's cycle and that of human beings. In the same way that the fetus already has drops of particles that would make it die in the end, the universe had its death within its creation. This is exactly why it was perceived that things come easily for nature, and in no way does its death occur as a surprise. Nature is ever ready. Nature practices predetermined duties. Nature never does anything other than what it has been designed to do.

To buttress this notion, Seneca identified some instances. The first was to sight the way a beach's wave turns over. That is, the ocean is designed to cause a flood naturally. The way the universe is already prepared for its death is an ideal figurative description of the way Seneca prescribed humans to live. An excerpt from his letter states that all activities that could possibly occur in the world can fit into one day. Awareness of this possibility helps maximize the advantage of the present.

A couple of days, months and years sum up a human being's entire life. However, they should not be seen from a futuristic angle; instead, they are similarly patterned circles revolving around the day which is present. As this day progresses from its beginning until its end, one can value it as having all things. If more days pass, there would simply be more days like the present. If every day is maximized to the fullest, one would have had enough time to get ready for death.

GOD

Studying nature and the heavens ultimately bring about the partial or even full understanding of God. Seneca classified God in different ways. He mentioned that God is what humans can and cannot see. It is impossible to think of any other thing that is as important as He is. God is all in all. He manages and controls His works internally and externally. He is the full reason and soul. He is the practical reason. Just as older Stoics believed, Seneca stressed that God could be called different names, such as nature, fate, providence, and even the universe. He also believed that God exists physically, and He is a big part of the universe. Furthermore, Seneca emphasized that human beings must see God through their thoughts, as He keeps eluding the human natural eyes. Hence, studying God is not a physical process. God and nature are of benefit to human beings.

Two of these aforementioned notions are specifically necessary for Seneca's ethical submissions. Quite a large part of On Benefits dwelled on the idea that God benefits human beings, and it is through the instance of how good God is that Seneca sought to discuss the reasons why giving does not have to be conducted to get something in return. God has absolutely nothing to benefit from human beings, yet He is beneficial to everyone. The biggest source of benefits is God. Being the reason behind all things, God is responsible for all the things human beings use to their advantage: the sun, the moon, rain, winter, and other seasons. This ultimately links with the idea that God has many names. Seneca imagined a possible objection that these natural blessings are what they are due to nature and not from God. However, such objections, according to him, would be misguided ones; nature is only another name for God.

Older theological practices in Stoicism were partially started through a contrasting distinction from the theological practices in Epicureanism. The core argument here is to ascertain whether God is concerned about humans, whether He cares to the extent of taking note of the patterns into which everyone's lives are shaped. Seneca apparently supported the traditional Stoic notion that God's care is in abundance. For instance, he explained that the manner through which God created the universe was like He had created an extremely good and firm building which thereafter had been gifted to humans.

Older Stoics posited that all human beings naturally preconceive the fact that there is a God and Seneca provided his own thoughts about it. He explained that rendering prayers would be tantamount to insanity had it been the case that God does not care about the human race. Human beings would be communicating only with deaf gods. According to Seneca, the fact that human beings in different parts of the world appear to always pray to God is an indication that He is real and, in fact, very caring.

In addition, Seneca supported the older Stoic practices in Physics which state the important implication of divination. In his explanation of the phenomena of thunder and lightning, Seneca said that these occurrences are signals of some things, but one should not believe God keeps Himself busy with such warnings so as to keep humans abreast of a specific situation. Humans should see these phenomena and try to find out what naturally causes them and come to an understanding that the sequence of all things is arranged by God. As long as this sequence exists, there would be genuine divination. Fate lends certainty to actions and occurrences, and nothing is capable of disrupting that. Even praying to God would not alter the dictates of fate.

However, because the gods omitted the natural provision of some things, prayer can fix those things. Just like other old philosophers, Seneca explained virtue as the notion of having similarities to God. However, it is not an overly spiritual notion. Instead, it is the notion of bringing one's rationality to perfection as being part of the entire universe. Human beings are basically pieces from God. Therefore, perfecting one's reasoning ability requires the perfection of the idea of divinity. In support of older Stoics, Seneca believed a man of virtue is at the same level as that of the gods. Seneca's natural theological and philosophical dispositions are very similar to his take on psychology and Ethics. In all, he was particular about the ways in which humans can bring their souls to perfection, and he strove to provide solutions to this notion in countless ways, such as explaining nature, virtue, theology, and the human soul.

IMPORTANT WORKS AND READING PRESCRIPTIONS

A distinct character evident in Seneca's participation is that he was the most interesting and engaging ancient philosopher. This is partly because many of his contributions had structures that resembled a letter. Consider the following recommendations.

On the Shortness of Life: This is a combination of three separate letters which best introduce readers to Seneca. The principal piece which explains the shortness of human lives is a severe notification of the fact that human beings' most valuable possession, time, can never be retrieved once it has been used. This piece is the source of one very prominent notion by Seneca. It states:

"We are not given a short life, but we make it short, and we are not Ill-supplied, but wasteful of it."

Seneca appears to have been a confidential friend who constantly encouraged his peers. His Letters can now be read as guides whenever one faces difficulties, anger, success, grief, failure, and other relevant areas of human endeavors.

LESSONS DERIVED FROM SENECA'S WORKS AND LIFE

Look for Support

In the letter written to Lucilius, Seneca encouraged him to find a reputable role model who would show him the principles by which to live. Although this notion is not strictly restricted to Stoic practices, Seneca explicitly explained the reason it is important to make such moves in one's struggle to have or live a good life. Such a role model would help make provisions for rules which can solve many critical and dangerous situations. Furthermore, the role model would ensure that one has a standard in which one must constantly measure up to and assess one's character daily.

Seneca stressed:
"So choose yourself a Cato—or, if Cato seems too severe for you, a Laelius, a man whose character is not quite so strict. Choose someone whose way of life, as well as words, and whose very face as mirroring the character that lies behind it, have won your approval. Be always pointing him out to yourself, either as your guardian or as your model. There is a need, in my view, for someone as a standard against which our characters can measure themselves. Without a ruler to do it against, you won't make crooked straight."

Do Not Be Enslaved by Wealth

This is contrasting ideas of wealth and philosophy. Nassim Taleb analyzed some useful ways to understand the nature of Seneca's riches. He said that Seneca desired the positive aspect of wealth and was always prepared to put it to use, but he never relied heavily on it. In fact, he controlled it in every sense. He took advantage of the positive aspects and completely snubbed the unpleasant ones. The need exists for persistent self-examination to ascertain whether one has been consumed with the luxury of being rich to the extent that one would become too afraid to live without it, thereby giving such luxuries the power to become one's controller.

Discussing his wealth in On the Happy Life, Seneca mentioned that a wise man would not see him as not meriting the proceeds or luxuries that accompany wealth. A wise man would not become affectionate with riches, but would nonetheless possess them. He would welcome them into his home, but not integrate them into his heart. He would never reject whatever belongs to him in terms of riches; rather, he would ensure they are kept. Finally, a wise man uses his wealth as a yardstick when putting his virtue into practice and regards riches as a slave. Seneca then wrapped up his description by emphasizing that only a fool would make wealth his or her master.

Your Ego Must Be Contained

Seneca understood the ways in which one's ego or pride can hinder one's development. The modern era is already plagued with unnecessary hype, and everyone tries to make one another consistently happy through hails and other forms of exaggerations. These heaped praises keep sinking into one's thoughts, and one begins to key into them. For instance, when an individual is constantly being referred to as a super human, if it is not adequately checked, he or she will subsequently begin to feel it is true. In a letter, Seneca preached to Lucilius to not be drawn into such situations.

He stressed that a huge challenge human beings face is that humans too easily get comfortable with themselves. As soon as one is called a good man with adoptable principles, one becomes flattered almost immediately. Individuals are not usually satisfied with precise and minimal praises but are quick to respond to exaggeration and unnecessary eulogies. Individuals are quick to agree with those who refer to them as wise, brave, or courageous, even when it is clear that such persons are untruthful.

Humans enjoy being praised so much that they wouldn't mind practicing a virtue that is largely contradictory to their actual habits. While an individual keeps instigating torture, he or she would still want to be seen as gracious. Hence, he or she would not see a need to desist from such acts, as he or she already assumes they are just.

Following are some popular quotes from Seneca.

"Think your way through difficulties: harsh conditions can be softened, restricted ones can be widened, and heavy ones can weigh less on those who know how to bear them."

"Let all your activity be directed to some object, let it have some end in view."

"Often a very old man has no other proof of his long life than his age."

"We say that nothing happens to the wise man against his expectation."

"Believe me, it is better to understand the balance-sheet of one's own life than of the corn trade."

"We are not given a short life, but we make it short, and we are not Ill-supplied but wasteful of it."

CHAPTER 9: CHRISTIANITY AND STOICISM

Notable traces of Stoic doctrines are in some Christian practices. The sentimental opinions some of the early Stoics shared whenever it came to talks on Christianity validate this. However, the two disciplines also have aspects in which they differ. The subsequent paragraphs will examine some of those points where they align, as well as those where they differ.

AFFINITIES: THE STOIC LOGOS AND CHRISTIANS' SERVITUDE

It is apparent that Stoicism and Christianity share an affinity in the way they view the notion of God. This is seen in their notions about acting according to the will of a supreme being. Christians and Stoics do not share a belief that a supreme being has the compulsory mandate to provide necessities, such as children and superfluous crop harvest. Rather, they have a similar notion that humans are to do the bidding of the supreme one and be of service to His dictates.

The early Stoics were known to have practiced monotheism. They shared Heraclitus' idea of "one Logos." They can be likened to growing a monotheistic practice found in Judaism, especially that which Moses had practiced earlier. Subsequently, Christians found a way to draw inferences from Stoicism. This is seen at the very beginning of St. John's gospel. In fact, against the rather popular take on Christianity, one could say that Stoicism showcases monotheism better than Christianity does, as it does not entertain negativity and does not treat issues such as demons or angels. Stoicism shares only the idea that there is one Logos.

On the notions of acting according to God's will and being of service to the Logos, Cleanthes wrote a piece which expresses his submission to the will of the Logos. This is like the Christians' Lord's Prayer. The two doctrines believe a feeling of fulfillment arises when one accepts the will of the supreme God. They believe the pattern of living enables human beings to be free from fear or anxiety. In other words, they would be courageous and bold in doing things in the right ways.

THE RESOUNDING IMPORTANCE OF WHO OR WHAT HUMANS SHOULD SERVE

Another notable similarity between Christianity and Stoicism is the notion of what matters most in life and the question of whom human beings serve and who their masters are. It is necessary to find answers to these questions because the two doctrines believe all the activities of human beings are reflections of whom or what they serve. Plato shared a similar idea, as he opined that if anyone approves their God publicly, they would instantly be enslaved by it and would have to play along with whatever the public dictates. Equally, should anyone idolize money, they would ultimately be enslaved by it acting according to its dictate.

THE ADOPTION OF INWARD SUBMISSION

Stoics and Christians also share a similar opinion on the idea of having a private relationship with whomever individuals consider to be God. They also both frown at the attention-seeking mode of service or worship because that would imply that such a person is being proud and showing gross disapproval for other people's choices. Epictetus explained that when one is thirsty, one should sip some water in his or her mouth and be quiet about it. Jesus also mentioned that Christians who try to draw the attention of others whenever they pray to God have already got their reward. Hence, nothing awaits them in the afterlife.

ASKESIS

Hadot once mentioned that Christians in the ancient world adopted the Stoic notion of askesis. This is the concept of developing a mind, a body, and desires that are spiritual in nature. Askesis was later reformed into asceticism by the desert fathers. It then became a comprehensive principle of disciplining oneself mentally and physically. This concept was widely relevant in traditional Christianity, which had its roots in Greek philosophy. However, modern forms of Christianity have caused a shift from this concept to that of an unnecessary admiration for Jesus. Recently, the cultivation of spiritual practices has begun gaining prominence in Christianity. Therefore, a chance exists that spiritual training would be reborn eventually.

PLACING GOD'S SERVICE ABOVE THE SERVICES RENDERED TO ANY MAN

The Stoic idea of Cosmopolis, which implies "a nation of God," can be said to have been reformed by Christianity. It is a notion that states an upright individual must place his service toward the cosmopolis above other things. Even his or her cultural beliefs or heritage must come below it. This notion is so important; it cuts across racial or tribal constraints and also emphasizes that all human beings have a unique God-like nature.

DIFFERENCES: THE HUMAN LOGOS

Christianity drew inferences from the Stoic notion of Logos. However, there are obvious differences between whom or what the two disciplines perceived as the Logos. It is glaring that serving a mysterious, unidentifiable being or Providence is not the same as worshiping an individual who came to the universe in human flesh, underwent trial and sufferings, and eventually died for his followers. Rationally, it becomes normal to be more emotionally attached to such physical representations than a pantheistic one the Stoics preached. An intellectual view might make one find it harder to accept the human Logos.

The Stoics' interactions with the Logos are quite different from the way Christians interact with God. The Stoics' connection with the Logos can be likened to that found between a father who is an aristocratic Roman and his offspring. To an extent, there is a gap; it is logical, understandable, and formed through an underlying concept of virtue and responsibility.

The Jewish Christianity extends well beyond that. It revolves around needs, emotions, constant arguments, and a God who is as needy as his worshipers. Then, the connection with God was an extensive, sensual, and emotional affair. A Christian God needed humans' affections, their praises, and had vowed to help humans who sought his assistance. Comparisons between Cleanthes' hymns, St Augustine's conversion tale, and David's hymns will immediately clarify this difference in how followers of the two disciplines relate to a supreme being.

THE EXTENSIVE NATURE OF CHRISTIANS' EMOTIONS AND NEEDS

To get a clearer understanding of the aforementioned, one must learn more about the needy and emotional structure that persists in Christianity. One can even argue that Christianity has more affinity with emotions and needs than Greek philosophy. On the one hand, it is dominated by groans, despair, anger, or sobs, and on the other hand, by extreme happiness and pleasure. Once more, the songs of David adequately explain and validate this. However, some practices in Christianity do not completely rely on emotions; this is especially common to Orthodox Christians. There are different forms of solicitations, pleas, and sentimental requests, such as: "Let us free," "We beg God," "Provide comfort," "Please listen" and so on. This is a huge contrast to the structure of the relationship that persists between the Stoics and "God." An instance is the Zeus statement that if anyone desires any good thing, such a person should get it by himself or herself.

THE DEPENDENCE ON GRACE

Epictetus stressed that, to a great extent, Christians are convinced that assistance from the Holy Spirit and God is certain. He explained that there is a common dependence on Grace, as well as its ability to assist humans and cause a positive turnaround in their lives. The Stoics believe that reasoning is from a supreme being, and assistance comes from individual reasoning and not directly from God.

THE EXISTENCE OF SATAN

Another important contrast is the notion of a great enemy of Christianity. Christians believe in the existence of a creature that rivals God's positive plans with negative ones. It is assumed that this evil has been empowered to control some activities in the universe and that these activities tend to tempt and bring about the destruction of human beings in the long run. This creature has many agents carrying out his bidding. In Stoic teachings, there are many instances in which the existence of an enemy is mentioned. However, the description of this enemy is not in any way related to the Christian one. Epictetus mentioned in one of his pieces that the human enemy is his bad behaviors and his lower self. In Roman Stoicism, the enemy is also equated to human beings' cruel parts, which are the contradictory aspects of their rather God-like nature.

This Christian notion reveals that the disciple views the world from a more complex perspective. A Christian sees the universe as occupied by dangers and satanic spirits whose aims are to bring about the destruction of the human race. However, a philosopher of Greek descent would note that these descriptions are grossly superstitious and can make sense only to a mad individual. Hardly was there a citation of demonic beings in Greek philosophy. The causes of sickness were believed to be negative thoughts and bad behaviors. From a therapeutic angle, this sort of approach is ideal if an anxious or depressed individual is informed that his or her situation is the result of some demonic beings, the individual's situation would only become worse.

It is understandable to find the Christians' belief in demons a bit archaic and intelligible. One cannot dispute that even Socrates appeared to have nursed such ideas. Stoics, on the other hand, have a notion that humans must pursue eudemonia, which implies a good demon. It is possible the Greek philosophy has an underlying blend of spirit-human relationship that most people seem to overlook. It is also likely that its naivety concerning the subject of evil relegated such beliefs into the background.

THE CONTRAST IN THE VIEWS OF HUMAN NATURE

The Christian belief in so-called "original sin" has created a feeling that humans have a nature of sinning. Hence, there is always a probability that humans would make mistakes that contradict the tenets of nature. Christianity preaches that human beings can make excuses for certain acts to create good impressions, but God is the one to ask for forgiveness and assistance with the knowledge that no one can be adequately perfect in the world. Greek philosophy dictates that human nature can be brought to perfection by good reasoning processes. It is believed that human beings are thinking beings, and everyone has been blessed with the ability to choose the exact way to live. Hence, human beings can be a Virtuoso, as well as Socrates in their approaches toward living.

The Christian story of the Garden of Eden might seem far-fetched to many in the modern world. However, its description of human beings appears to be more plausible than that of Aristotle or Socrates. This is because the population of human beings who are supposed to follow the dictates of nature rationally is very minute. The universe is otherwise filled with humans who struggle to make amends for repeated mistakes. Human beings can be likened to a sort of flower in many millions of blossoms.

CERTAINTY OF A LIFE AFTER NOW

Christianity's take on a life beyond the one in which human beings currently exist is resoundingly strong, much more than how Stoics perceive the notion. Although this idea has gone through refinements over time and has integrated into comprehensive ecclesiastic studies, Christians have a strong belief that the human body resurrects after death and either remains in heaven or hell forever. Old Catholic teachings also stress the idea of purgatory. Stoics are not certain about the existence of such a life. It is hardly mentioned in their teachings. Reincarnation was mentioned by Plato, even though it lacked depth and comprehensiveness.

In addition, Christians believe that although human nature is imperfect and has many shortcomings, the redemption of souls would occur at a supposed "end of days" as Jesus made his way back to the universe. By contrast, Stoics hold the opinion that things would progress the way they are until a cosmic conflagration occurs and then the universe would be reset once more.

The two notions are a bit arbitrary, but the advent of astrophysics has lent a form of prominence to the Stoic theory as the possibility of some major disasters has been predicted. A crucial contrast between modern Christianity and Stoicism is the fact that Stoics now appear to be atheists due to the negligence of the notion of providence or Logos, even though they still stress the need to apply rationality in everything. Therefore, one can say that Stoicism cuts across different religions. Its principles can be employed by anyone.

CHRISTIANITY HAS A BIGGER RECEPTION AND COMMUNITY

Christianity thrives on music, dance, myths, and other aspects that blend with modern human beings' opinions about the world. It grew rapidly and became a worldwide religion. Christianity relates to emotions, intellect, the human body, and the motivation to appreciate God and the gift of life. This also explains why many of those who teach philosophical ideas still find themselves attached to one religion or another.

LOVE CONQUERS RATIONALITY IN CHRISTIANITY

While Stoics perceive an insane human as unfit and lesser than others, Christianity perceives everyone as equal, race and deformity notwithstanding. This idea has greatly fostered the viability and adoption of Christianity in the sense that communities thrive when they are built on love and not the Stoic notion of rationality. The latter brings about hierarchy and strictness, which human beings would naturally find hard to deal with.

CHAPTER 10: MODERN STOICISM

The attempt to modernize Stoicism began in the late 20th and early 21st Centuries. It was, at the time, a popular and intelligible advancement that sought to enliven Stoic practices in the modern world. Modern Stoicism is not the same as Neostoicism, which occurred in the 17th Century. Modern Stoicism spread across the renewal of attention, as well as the philosophical attempts to realign early Stoicism with current or recent concepts and ideologies. In 2012, modern Stoicism received a boost in the aspects of acceptability, recognition, and interest due to the launch of the yearly "Stoic Week" program.

ANTECEDENTS

The sudden increase in interest in the study of virtue and Ethics as a whole created the development of modern Stoicism. Contributions by staunch philosophers, such as Martha Nussbaum, Alasdair MacIntyre, Philippa Foot, and a few others gave prominence to virtue once more as opposed to the previous domination by the consequentialist and deontological notions. The increase in the production of books concerning early Stoicism during the early stages of the 21st Century greatly influenced the emergence of modern Stoicism. This was because many of the old works underwent appropriate translations to enhance the comprehension of modern scholars. The foundation of modern Stoicism was laid by Dr. Albert Ellis, who was responsible for the development of Rational Emotive Behavior Therapy. Aaron T. Beck is another foundational figure in this field. He was also known to have been the proponent of earlier editions of Cognitive Behavioral Therapy. Viktor Frankl made good use of Stoic principles in the World War. He later founded the concept of logotherapy.

Lawrence Becker expressed a thought about how intriguing it would have been if Stoicism's reign had continued for another 2,300 years after it was first introduced. He stated that it would be good to have witnessed what would have occurred if its notions had to go against the likes of Darwin, Kant, Marx, Bacon, Newton, Descartes, Locke, and Hobbes, etc. This idea can be said to have formed a crucial part of the foundation of modern Stoicism. It is little wonder that Lawrence's book, A New Stoicism, continues to serve as a reference point for modern Stoic practices.

STOICISM AS AN ANTECEDENT FOR PSYCHOTHERAPY

Psychotherapy in the modern world was arguably inspired by the Stoic philosophy, as can be seen in Albert Ellis' explanation of Rational Emotive Behavior (REB) therapy. In addition, Aaron Beck's piece on cognitive therapy pointed out the fact that the origin of the philosophy of cognitive therapy can be found in the works of Stoic philosophers. In fact, Ellis and others used a quote from Epictetus' handbook at the beginning of REB therapy sessions.

The famous quote stressed the fact that occurrences on their own are not responsible for a human being's anger. Rather, the opinions human beings have concerning such occurrences are to be held responsible. The notion formed a prominent feature in the socialization stage of other techniques in Cognitive Behavioral Therapy. Stoicism's relevance in recent psychotherapy treatments was explained extensively by Donald Robertson in his book Philosophy of Cognitive Behavioral Therapy. A notable institution greatly influenced by Stoicism is the Rational Persuasion School, which was created by Paul Dubois, a Swiss psychotherapist who practiced in the 20th Century. He made constant references to Stoicism as he advised those who consulted with him to read excerpts from Seneca's works during their private time.

POPULARITY

An important aspect of modern Stoicism is its globalization. Its heavy use of social media platforms aided the popularity and the spread of the movement. Scott (E.O.) once mentioned that modern Stoicism could be described as a Web 2.0 success. Moreover, the Stoicism Today blog, the online Annual Stoic Week, and the offline Stoicon program have all contributed to the advancement of modern Stoicism. Equally, the New Stoa, a Stoic community created in 1996, is said to have contributed immensely to the development of modern Stoicism. It remains the longest functioning Stoicism website.

A few blogs explore Stoic views, and some of these platforms are owned by renowned scholars, such as John Sellars, and William Irvine, among others. Therapists such as Donald Robertson also own blogs where they integrate Stoic practices into their views. Scott opined that the increase in the growth of modern Stoicism has been because of social media publicity, constant articles, and the numerous books that have been published.

Many group meeting spots exist for Stoics and Stoicism enthusiasts in London, Dublin, New York, Toronto, Denver, Australia, Manchester, and many other places. The Stoicism Group page on Facebook is another very important platform that has influenced Stoicism greatly. It has more than 27,000 subscribers. Similarly, more than 53,000 users are included in its Reddit group. Apart from the sites that use English as their primary language, a few converse in other languages, such as German and Russian.

It is not an exaggeration to say that many industries apply modern Stoic principles in their administrations and practices. An article published by Forbes once declared that some thoughts from modern Stoicism appear to be promising, especially for political leaders and businesses that face challenges. In addition, the efficiency of Stoic principles in battling depression continues to gain more recognition.

IDEOLOGIES: CONSTRAINTS ON THE NOTION OF NATURE

The ancient Stoic principle of acting according to the dictates of nature has constantly met multiple challenges in modern Stoicism. Early Stoics stressed the idea that there is no other way to live a good life apart from dancing to the tune of nature. They believed nature is perfect and all things that conform to it are equally ideal. Furthermore, they held a strong opinion about teleology. They shared the idea that all the occurrences within the universe have been pre-designed for specific reasons and they all eventually add up to positive outcomes.

In the modern era, this view is rather hard to support. Becker once stated that the emergence of advanced science had posed so many questions to the metaphysical notions of the Stoics that everyone seriously doubts the concept of the sequential organization of life's events in the current century. Becker clarified that when human beings interact with the world, they fight against its nonchalance to them, as well as their lack of importance to it. He emphasized that the universe doesn't notice any human being; it has not actually laid-down rules that human beings are to adopt. More worrying are the saddening events that have plagued the modern world. Increased incidences of murder, suicide, manslaughter, genocide, and many other gruesome occurrences perpetrated by humans pose challenges to the initial Stoic notion that the universe has been rationally organized.

There are even bigger issues with which to contend should human nature be put under focus. Becker stated that while it is normal to discover ideal patterns of character in human behavior and approaches, the tendency to come across multiple contrasting characteristics cannot be ruled out. Due to this, human characteristics cannot be used as a viable reference in ethical arguments concerning nature. For instance, if, by nature, human beings are A and there is a B whose nature contradicts A, the result would be that B contradicts human beings' nature. In addition, if A is what determines the importance of human beings, to grow successfully as a human being, one must be very good at A. Accepting the idea of human nature does not mean there is a particular guide to use. Modern Stoicism is faced with this issue, and it boils down to the fact that it is very complex to establish ethical concepts on the basis of nature, even when it is universal or cosmic.

THE REFORMATION OF THE "FOLLOWING NATURE" NOTION

Becker had suggested that the eradication of the "follow nature" concept would help improve Ethics in Stoicism. He hinted that the notion had been so comprehensively integrated into Stoic practices that it may prove impossible to erase it completely. A good solution, then, is to change its interpretation. He suggested that following nature should mean taking after facts. This also means humans are expected to find viable things concerning the social and the physical world. It is also important to get the details of one's condition within it before one makes some decisions about typical or standard issues. Following nature should now be seen as confronting the facts, taking them as they appear without any form of addition or subtraction before one makes any decision. It also implies practicing Ethics through facts and the construction of standard propositions. It implies amending the standard propositions to blend with the subsequent evolution of such facts and, ultimately, taking the amendments as they are without excuses or additions. Becker also opined that following nature should be referred to as living in alignment with the facts, reveling in reality instead of an imaginary standard.

Science helps obtain facts concerning the universe. Becker mentioned that social sciences, biological sciences, and behavioral sciences all help Ethics in some crucial ways. At first, they provide materials that can be employed during realistic debates. They provide detailed explanations that assist in distinguishing between permanent behaviors and temporary ones. Again, they provide important, comprehensive, and detailed explanations of rationality, learning, and making choices.

A Stoic cannot successfully process Ethics without the availability of some important suggestions, representations, or descriptions. That is, Stoics need empirical verification. Empirical verification can be achieved through a scientific process. In a way, the idea of "taking after facts" is not necessarily one that contradicts science. However, it should not be mistaken for "adopting science," as that would reduce the scope of the idea and mislead human beings. This implies that a modern Stoic would not remove the necessity of getting his or her children protected from diseases.

AGENCY, VIRTUE, AND HAPPINESS

Becker summed up all his knowledge of Ethics in Stoicism under the idea of agency. He stated that the ideal agency helps develop virtue accordingly. This means a need exists to approach the subject of virtue with the utmost importance when one seeks to get the best from one's agency. Agency is described as an equilibrium between stability and control, carrying out activities after careful consideration of all attached aspects. That is, agency is put into action once comprehensive facts have been provided.

Becker viewed happiness as derivable from agency. He emphasized that according to experienced and suitable agents, happiness can be viewed as a characteristic of the entirety of human lives and not just a temporary mental phenomenon. Happiness can be derived from an adequate balance of control in the activities of agency. This form of happiness seems to be a psychological product of standard agency and implies that a staunch Stoic's life is dominated by that form of happiness as a product of the virtue he constantly practices.

LEVELS OF VIRTUE

Becker's brand of Stoicism constantly questioned many of the beliefs that early Stoics held. For instance, the strict adoption of virtue as the ideal way to live received continuous criticism. Traditional Stoics did not leave room for a lukewarm approach in the practice of Stoicism. One is either a Stoic Sage or a non-Stoic. There was no form of level or degree to which anyone could practice Stoicism. However, Becker prescribed a rather subtle and slightly different appraisal of the subject. He stressed that human beings could drown reaching the deepest part of the sea and then be positioned at the bottom of it all. This is why modern Stoics believe that some early Stoic doctrines cannot be successfully defended in the face of criticisms.

THE UNIVERSALITY QUEST

Another point that modern Stoics have contemplated is the ancient Stoic notion that Stoic practices extend to all human beings and represent the only ideal way to live one's life. In New Stoicism, Becker argued that behaving according to those tenets as laid down by ancient Stoics is a sort of noble project, but the tenets will likely be rejected by some individuals. People with attributes such as addiction, obsession, and compulsion would have a hard time trying to follow these prescriptions by ancient Stoics. Modern Stoics believe that only those whose deliberations are fitting can willingly accept such principles or doctrines.

ARISTOTLE AND STOICISM

The differences between ancient and modern Stoic practices also extend to an inquisition concerning the influence of external goods in molding the lives of human beings. A traditional Stoic believes that living and leading a good life does not require any form of initial advantage. Human beings can become sages under any circumstance. Illness, physical disability, or even poverty does not undermine anyone's capability. Before the modern era, the view had been heavily criticized by Aristotelians who believed that a measure of good helps foster the practice of virtue. Becker somewhat supports the latter notion. He opined that physical and mental health would always be an important part of an individual's development in all aspects of life. Once a part gets dented, there would be a corresponding dent in the development capability of agency.

THE DICHOTOMY IN THE CONCEPT OF CONTROL

Ancient Stoicism extensively analyzed the differences between occurrences that can be managed by human beings and those that cannot. Although this idea has received a good reception from modern Stoics, others have still managed to re-translate it. Becker said that the entire idea of this distinction has been oversimplified. He clarified that the difference between those activities that human beings can successfully manage and those humans could not manage is confusing. Becker stated that it is preferable that humans check and adjust their strengths and try to balance them with the fragile or transient nature of the particular events or objects in focus.

William Irvine approached the description of the Dichotomy by stating that dividing occurrences into things human beings can or cannot control is too strict. He stated that there should be another point to consider; notion ought to be in three parts. Irvine argued that Epictetus' idea that some events are completely out of the control of human beings. Vice versa is a faulty one because he left out the possibility of events over which human beings have partial control.

Pigliucci explained that some occurrences are dependent on human actions and decisions. Other events, such as natural phenomena and the history of a sect, cannot be said to be the doings of any particular individual. However, human beings are partially capable of controlling a few events. This last exception depends on human beings' personal aims.

RENUNCIATION AND ASKESIS

No evident relationship exists between the definition of a Sage's belief concerning the normal inherent pleasure that life has to offer and the evaluation of ascetic traits in Stoicism.

Becker explained that the difficulty faced by Stoics and critics alike in the interpretation of the Stoic notion is that an ideal life is lived without the benefits of pleasures, such as food, music, sex, friends, and fame, among others. It stems from the fact that the early Stoics used the eudemonic life of a Sage as a substitute for normal happiness. This is also why Stankiewicz tried to amend the ascetic notion by stating that it has been widely misinterpreted. He stressed that Stoicism is not the same as Asceticism and Stoics cannot be compared to monks. He also emphasized that Epicureans are more abstemious than Stoics will ever be; the notion is far more elaborate, and it cannot be equated with asceticism. Modern Stoics can decide to diversify, be very sensual, exhibit lushness, and succeed in the world by taking things as they are. In contrast to the life a monk leads, Stoics do not ignore the large number of diverse sensualities that life has to offer.

The aforementioned position was subsequently refuted by Kevin Patrick, who asserted that such interpretations exemplify hedonism. It is also the same as other regular, incorrect interpretations. Stankiewicsz's interpretation simply means that because external events are not directly linked to humans, everyone can lust after all the things he or she desires. Patrick finalized his dispute by stating that modern Stoics must live precisely like Stoics.

Irvine posited a rather modest position creating the concept of Voluntary Discomfort. He explained that allowing oneself to pass through discomforts, such as choosing to starve when one could get meals to fill one's stomach, is a way of preparing for an unforeseen difficulty that may occur later. If human beings were to be conversant with only comfort, the consequences of a highly probable difficulty might be grave and costly. Discomforts that are voluntary are like vaccines. They would help resist – as well as create an immune system against – imminent problems that would arise as time went by.

CHAPTER 11: THE RESOUNDING IMPORTANCE OF STOICISM

The resident knowledge in Stoicism cannot be overestimated. In fact, the world as we know it today must make use of its teachings more often than they are currently being used, as these teachings or tenets have been responsible for some very crucial human practices. Following are a few aspects in which Stoic practices should not be overlooked.

CREATED FOR DIFFICULT SITUATIONS

At the time of its introduction, the world, as scantily populated as it was then, was already on the verge of collapse. Stoicism was created many years after the untimely death of Alexander, an event that shook the Greek world. Stoic teachings soon became acceptable because they provided stability, peace, and security in a period when the world was rocked by a crisis. Stoic principles did not propose a form of peace or security that could be enjoyed only after death. Instead, Stoics prescribed ways in which humans could live happily while they were physically alive.

Stoic teachings posited that things prone to destruction or change do not possess the power to give long-lasting happiness. For instance, human careers might be prosperous or otherwise, relations could be lost or begin, monetary accounts may or may not increase. All these events cannot give genuine happiness. The inner mind is that single location which external events do not have the ability to overpower. This is because human beings have the sole power to choose, process thoughts, and act appropriately.

Even though the universe is capable of externally retracting good things from an individual, Stoicism makes everyone understand that he or she has an inherent gift that supersedes other things. Epictetus, a staunch Stoic philosopher who was born into slavery and subsequently became a cripple, once stated that good is in the will of every individual. Unhappiness is only a judgment made and reasoning adopted by the unhappy individual – nothing more.

Although it is understandable that pain would cause any human to react, a Stoic is taught to remain unshaken about all the things that occur externally and to remain contented during harsh or blissful times. It is a tasking requirement, but Stoicism offers a life that would be completely free from desires and feelings which, on many occasions, control human beings when it should actually be the other way around. A genuine Stoic is not without feelings. Rather, he or she has been able to manage his or her emotions successfully. This is because Stoic practices dictate that grief, fear, or avarice can creep into the human mind only when they are given permission.

Hence, these sorts of principles are as applicable to a world on the verge of chaos as they are to the financial crisis in which the modern world keeps finding itself. Epictetus mentioned that the world would always be thrown into chaos if what human beings do is try to derive happiness from destructible things.

STOICISM STRIVES FOR GLOBALIZATION

Stoicism was discovered in a universe where human beings had parochial inclinations. Many human beings believed strongly in old religious practices, the spirit of nationality, and the importance of recognition and status. Stoicism remains the only cogent reason those sorts of beliefs are largely strange and incomprehensible in the modern world. It was arguably the foremost philosophical school to put universality into effective practice. Epictetus explained that every human being is a citizen of his immediate community, but is also an integral part of bigger cities of God and men. Marcus Aurelius stressed that the need exists to continuously learn ways to appreciate the entire world, just as one appreciates and values his community. He also mentioned that as long as human beings are responsible for making themselves happy, there will hardly be any division among different social settings. Seneca, who lived in a city dominated by slaves, asked the Romans to remember that those whom they called slaves were covered by the same sky as they were, breathed the same way they did, and would live and die the same way they would. The integration of the notion of "the cosmos," which was translated as "worldwide city," gave Stoicism the status of a reasonable philosophy in Rome. Stoicism also helped create a platform for interactions among a large number of individuals from different backgrounds. It, therefore, played an important role in globalization. It has not ceased doing so.

BEING A CHRISTIAN MEANS BEING A PARTIAL STOIC

Christianity is a religion that emphasizes cordial human relations and has also been seen as being controlled by a kind supreme being, God. It preaches that human beings must learn to live above their natural urges instead of being consumed by them. However, due to inherent human nature, Christian teachings express the belief that human beings are liable to experience some shortcomings. Christianity also dwells extensively on the issue of conscience and the diverse abilities of an inestimable God. While all these concepts appear common, the ideas were brought to life through Stoicism.

That Christianity has its roots in Stoicism is very reasonable. Stoicism reigned in the Roman Empire for a long period. This is the same nation where Christianity came to the fore. Many ancient Christian leaders were once Stoics. Many terminologies in Christianity were taken from Stoicism. This is because thoughts and talks concerning religion at the time were centered mostly on the Stoic practices. When the religion began to expand in popularity and acceptability, its leaders reduced their connection to Stoicism because they had to publicize the Christian faith. However, Stoicism remains an integral part of Christianity when some of its notions and terminologies are brought into focus.

A PHILOSOPHY FOR THE MILITARY

James Stockdale's Skyhawk was brought down in 1965. What he remembered that moment after he was ejected, is that he had only a few seconds to utter words before his freedom was seized. He stated that all he could utter was that he would be kept from technology and go into a world like that of Epictetus.

Stockdale was in captivity for about eight years, and he penned his gratitude for how Stoicism preserved his dear life. Before being deployed, he had devoted quality time to studying Stoic ideas and practices, and the knowledge assisted him in enduring struggles while in captivity. He mentioned that an expression by Epictetus repeatedly rang in his ears. He had opined that a soldier's service is equivalent to life itself. When a soldier absconds from his duties, he has brought the entire army to a sympathetic position. As many his prison mates taunted one another by giving untrue intuitions that they would be released early, Stockdale's Stoic perceptions helped him face the unpleasant reality of his capture and drained any form of depression or fright.

Stockdale was not the only soldier to have fortified himself with Stoic principles when the need arose. Nancy Sherman, a renowned philosophy teacher at the Naval Academy, emphasized in her book, The Stoic Warrior, that Stoic notions serve immensely as a catalyst for a military mind construct, particularly in situations such as endurance, strength, and self-control. Sherman noted that as soon as her class focused on the Stoics, many of her students instantly believed they had been brought home.

RELEVANCE TO LEADERSHIP

Stoicism dictates that before one tries to be in charge of some occurrences, one must be able to control oneself. An individual's strive to become influential in the universe is prone to constraints, such as failure, missed opportunities, and disappointments. However, inward control is sure to yield positive and successful results. From the period of Marcus Aurelius' reign, leaders have discovered that practicing some Stoic principles gives them a form of regard to unpleasant situations. Moreover, the principles assist in curbing pride when humans face favorable situations.

Stoicism attracts individuals who have been troubled by uncertainties. Because leaders, on most occasions, are exposed to constant changes and risks, a good number of them understand that the importance of Stoic principles to their psychological construct cannot be overestimated.

For instance, Barack Obama's Stoic behavior was depicted while he was being interviewed by Michael Lewis. He told Lewis that he had begun to reduce the way he made decisions because he no longer wanted to be responsible for deciding what he would eat or what he would wear. Obama stressed that one must put oneself on a routine, as it was not advisable to be distracted daily with trivial information. This assertion portrays Obama as a practicing Stoic because he was able to successfully identify those things that can be considered important and unimportant on different levels in life.

Truth be told, practicing Stoic principles does not mean one will always get positive outcomes. Even though no one would perceive Bill Clinton as a Stoic, Marcus' Meditations is one of Clinton's favorites. Cato the Younger supported the philosophy for most of his life. Yet, he was constantly associated with vices such as drunkenness and violence resulting from uncontrollable anger and pride, among others. Yet whenever he exhibited his bravery, especially when he defeated Caesar's army, Cato acted according to Stoic principles.

Stoicism emphasizes that human beings experience failures more often than successes. Being human means being angry, self-centered, and scared on more occasions than anyone could fathom. Nonetheless, Stoics also provide practicable ways to be better humans. Continuous practice of Stoic principles in favorable conditions would foster their effective use whenever the situation warrants it.

CHAPTER 12: STOIC PRINCIPLES

UNDERSTAND THAT EMOTIONS ARE FROM THE INNER MIND

"Today I escaped anxiety. Or no, I discarded it, because it was within me, in my own perceptions — not outside." - Meditations (Marcus Aurelius)

External occurrences or circumstances are not responsible for making one feel a certain thing. One's feeling is informed by whatever one has personally told himself or herself. A plain canvas, a sheet, or untouched notes and lists are not complex. One's thoughts constitute the complexity of one's life. Quite a number of human beings are prone to shifting responsibilities and condemnations on physical things because the task is very easy to carry out. The reality is that disagreements or contradictions begin inwardly from one's mind. Absconding from facts, urgent calls, or emails, and other necessities would do nothing but bring harm to oneself and ultimately take away one's discipline.

When one comes face to face with a challenge, one shouldn't find comfort in the physical circumstances. Instead, one should look inwardly and reach for one's genuine stance. External circumstances do not contribute to one's feeling about a thing. Rather, one's body feeds on whatever the mind has proposed and created a feeling through that.

Move close to a respectable individual so that he or she can be a yardstick for your honesty. Find an individual who lives, preaches, acts, and behaves in a way that aligns with one's perception and whose face reflects his true character. In other words, one should always identify him either as one's role model or one's guardian. It is important to have a person whose own ethical standard can constantly be used to measure one's own. A crooked line cannot be straightened without the introduction and use of a ruler (an extract from Seneca's Letter from a Stoic).

No matter what one does for a living, there are resourceful personalities from whom one can always acquire knowledge. One can delve into the study of their works, approaches, skills, triumphs, and downfalls. Written and recorded pieces about these sorts of individuals have been made available. One can even go ahead and send them direct emails to get the best of them. Subsequently, one will learn the processes that sum up their achievements and use such techniques for one's personal life.

It should be noted that this form of emulation should not be seen as making a comparison. If one's service or product does not get to the spotlight on time or if, as a writer, one is unable to get a good book deal in many months as one's chosen model, it does not in any way suggest that one has failed or lived below fulfillment. Instead, the questions to ask are: How can one gain knowledge from one's role model? In what ways do their preaching and recommendations assist in one's growth and learning processes? Notwithstanding anyone's status or position in the world, they always have mentors and models to take after.

UNDERSTANDING THAT LIFE CONTINUES AFTER FAILURE

One's experiences should not stop one from being generous, sane, humble, and prudent, or from exercising self-control and other good habits which would naturally assist in living a fulfilled life. Whenever a situation or an event means to bring pain and suffering into one's life, one must understand that the occurrences are not without their good sides. In fact, they have been designed to occur so that one's ability to overcome them will earn one great fortune. One can devote a couple of months or even years on a project or business and still receive heavy criticism of it thereafter. Subsequently, one would begin feeling unmotivated and depressed. Even when failure keeps one in such conditions, the process of bouncing back to one's best is a noble practice and the lessons that one would learn from such activities ultimately help one become a better human being. The idea is that without failure, there would not be any growth.

Study with purpose and put your knowledge into prompt action. It is not enough to study writings or texts; one must exhibit whatever one has learned through one's outstanding thoughts, new approaches to things, and polished reflective abilities. Generally, texts help train the reader's mind. They are usually useful, although it would be an error to assume that development has occurred in one's life simply by digesting the contents inwardly.

For instance, studying books that discuss creativity, trading or banking will create endless opportunities for one to develop and make advancements. The effectiveness of such studies lies in the ability to practice the acquired knowledge. Studying prepares one's mind and prevents one from taking the wrong steps. In the end, studying can be seen only through actions that may yield success or failure, or produce an important lesson.

The main aim of education is to acquire knowledge inwardly. However, the inward knowledge is expected to spring up actions and foster one's decision-making processes. Studying some self-help texts would instantly inspire one to make certain changes, but the question remains: Do we adopt the principles learned when we face circumstances such as dealing with rude individuals, strangers, or bullies?

CONTINUOUSLY PUSH THE BOUNDARIES OF YOUR HONESTY

Crucial progress toward salvation is becoming personally aware of one's improper actions. This is because it is impossible to listen to corrections if one is not aware of the fact that one is in the wrong lane. It is important to feel guilty about a situation so that reforms can begin. In fact, some individuals would stand up to boast about their failures. Is there any way in which an individual who perceives his flaws as deserving praise would have possibly thought about the way forward?

One's best capability highlights the guilt one feels. It is important to carry out personal findings on all the facts that must have been presented against one. One should assume the role of prosecutor, judge and accused. It is important to not be soft on oneself in some situations. For instance, it is not possible to turn over a new leaf if one is not sure about the reasons one decided not to work, but see movies on a daily basis.

One should always be aware of the things that prevent one from being active, showing commitment, and getting busy. One should constantly ask, "What is responsible for the way I am?" Finding the right answers to this question is of utmost importance. Constant repetition of such questions would motivate one until one gets to the bottom of it all. The difficulty in this practice lies in one's ability to successfully process such forms of thoughts.

Natural gifts or spontaneity do not matter much here.

Practicing self-consciousness – being aware of one's thoughts and how one feels and acts – requires strength. Consistent practices keep self-consciousness stronger.

THINK ABOUT THE THINGS THAT CONSUME MOST OF YOUR TIME

It is important to note that the value of attentiveness is at varied levels and is in relation to circumstances. Hence, trivial things should not consume more than they should. In other words, those who purposely say negative things about others should not receive any form of attention. The best action to take is to ignore them completely. Indeed, those who perform excellently at their work, as well as those who are seen as masters in their fields, are what they are because they were able to place their priorities on those things for which they were known. They ensured that every hour of each day was not wasted on trivialities. The questions are: If we are to monitor our role models closely through a camera, is it certain that our paces at work will measure up? Will we be as focused and determined as they are when trying to put things in place?

A regular human being finds himself busy with the activities in other people's lives – social media browsing, for instance. Although it is ideal to take some occasional breaks during the day, it is important to manage one's distractions adequately.

ALWAYS BE CONSCIOUS THAT PROCRASTINATION IS NOT IDEAL

Starting a project might seem troublesome, but this extract may be of help.
"At dawn, when you have trouble getting out of bed, tell yourself: I have to go to work – as a human being. What do I have to complain about if I'm going to do what I was born for

181

– the things I was brought into the world to do? Or is this what I was created for? To huddle under the blankets and stay warm?"

Do you think you came into the world only to feel "good" without participating and having experiences? We should always be concerned with the activities of birds, spiders, bees, and even ants, carrying out consistent tasks, doing their best to ensure their responsibilities and quota are met. It would be unacceptable if we are not ready to carry out expected tasks. It is important always to pursue what nature has bestowed on us. Sure, we must rest on some occasions. However, nature has set a limit on the number of hours we should sleep, just as it has put restrictions on food and drink intake. Even with that, every human has had enough of such luxuries, working excluded. This means one's responsibility has not been carried out to its maximum. It means one does not value oneself to the optimum, and that extends to one's love for nature. Those who are in love and are dedicated to the things they usually do will not retire until they are completely tired. Many such individuals would not even remember eating. It is hardly possible for a regular human being to have more passion for nature in the way an engraver makes his engravings, or the passion showed by a political aspirant when trying to increase his post. As soon as all these individuals become engrossed with their work, they can refuse to eat, drink, or sleep and simply continue to engage in their works.

DO AWAY WITH THE GADGET AND LIVE IN THE PRESENT

Seneca expressed in his Letters from a Stoic, *"Nothing, to my way of thinking is a better proof of a well-ordered mind than a man's ability to stop just where he is and pass some time in his own company."*

It is not correct to think we are in an era in which people get distracted easily. Instead, it is an era in which adults have failed to instill the culture of embracing inward thoughts to the younger ones. There is no difference between a child who has decided to play games on her tablet in a restaurant and an adult who consistently flicks through Instagram while his or her friends are present. Those periods should be for communication, connection, or interaction with those physically present. Living in the present and trying to live privately can be cultivated. Some humans have been able to master it because they have created time to do so. To be candid, they could become insane if they were forced to do without such a lifestyle. It is important to find the time within a day, no matter how tight one's schedule, to remain seated and be calm for some moments. It should be done without any consideration of the external environment. One should breathe deeply for some seconds, put one's phone on "silent" so as to avoid being distracted, and begin thinking about all the events that occurred in one's day.

While at work, it is important to be persistently alert. One's mind should be fixed on current projects and what they are ultimately bound to yield. Such projects or tasks should be carried out carefully, attentively, and diligently. In the long run, one would realize the quality of personal improvement that has been achieved as well as how such activities have added to one's creativity. One's life, in general, would have greatly appreciated in value.

REMIND YOURSELF THAT TIME IS OUR MOST PRECIOUS RESOURCE

Always remember that time remains the most valuable possession.

"Not to live as if you had endless years ahead of you. Death overshadows you. While you're alive and able — be good." — Marcus Aurelius, Meditations.

A particularly interesting concept about Stoicism is that notions about death are relatively dominant in its preaching. Stoics are very aware of the transient nature of humans and how this is replicated in different aspects of life. A sense of urgency is awoken instantly as soon as one realizes that one has been living in the world for so many hours, and the hours left to spend are not in any way as certain as the ones already spent. When this idea is understood, one becomes aware that each day presents an opportunity to make improvements to sincerely value all the things one has learned, and that one is accountable for one's life.

This lends importance to one's generous habits, attentiveness, work orientations, self-discipline, and overall development. No one would want to exit life battling with "had I known." Therefore, Stoic principles may shape one's life into a good structure. They lead one to become motivated and humble.

Seneca stated, *"We should hunt out the helpful pieces of teaching and the spirited and noble-minded sayings which are capable of immediate practical application – not far-fetched or archaic expressions or extravagant metaphors and figures of speech – and learn them so well that words become works."*

The pattern in which one directs and lives one's life should always reflect one's chosen principles. It should dwell less on criticisms, consumption, and comparisons, and more on learning conscious living and consistent creativity. We should not be deceived by mere impressions. It is necessary to unravel the facts beyond the surface level.

A quick flashback to the moment a certain tragic event would always stir up emotions. Almost immediately, feelings of anger or hatred would creep in. This means one has let one's emotions dictate such conditions as well as determine one's response. Such emotional reactions cannot be escaped naturally as they are a vital aspect of human biology. The Stoics preached that human beings could substitute such emotions with reasonable thoughts. Just like a very fine wine is initially perceived as being merely a composition of grape fermentation, humans can eliminate the seemingly untrue aspects of some events and reveal their true form through an objective approach. It is through this procedure that one would be able to adopt appropriate responses. We can take breaks, breathe deeply, and try to understand our emotional reactions. Hence, we can distinguish the occurrence from our responses to realize that we can manage our emotions in that situation. We can generate expressions such as: *"That bad thing happened? Yes, but this situation is outside me."*

It is ideal to pay attention to the things within one's capacity and be less bothered about other things beyond us. Would it be ideal to become angry because it rained despite the forecast's prediction of a sunny day? Is there a need to be furious that the forecaster did not correctly predict that the sun would refuse to rise as it should have?

Life, in general, is as uncontrollable as the weather. Other's opinions, habits, actions, and occurrences that happen around us are largely beyond our control. In place of unnecessary fretting, we must learn to admit that there are things we cannot alter. The things on which we should most focus are things within our capabilities, actions, and thoughts.

One's health may improve if one has daily exercise and healthy eating. Nonetheless, disease may still creep into one's system. This is beyond one's control. It is important to focus on the things within one's power as this will afford one the chance to take advantage of situations and advance steadily toward one's aims.

Accept every occurrence with an honest mind. Nature's manifestation cannot be altered. One is bound to face many challenging situations in life. Although one's actions and thought patterns might be within one's control, the challenges one faces are not usually within one's power. Humans can be viewed as mere threads in the continuously evolving fabric of the universe.

Challenges should be confronted without laxities. There is no need to try to change the course of nature. Rather, one should find opportunities in every situation to put one's Stoic Ethics and virtues into practice. In line with this, Epictetus narrated the tale of Agrippinus, who had begun to prepare for his lunch but was stunned as a man brought the news that he had been exiled by Nero. Unperturbed, he responded swiftly, "We should just take the lunch to Arica then."

REFLECT ON YOUR LIFE'S STANDARD – THE MIND IS PURIFIED THROUGH HUMILITY

In most cases, human beings are dazed by the events that occur from time to time in life. As one interacts with family, school peers, and colleagues at work, one tends to completely overlook all other existing things beyond one's circle of experience. It is important to always spend time reflecting on one's life and blending with one's current environment before progressing to the community, then the city. After that stage, one can move further to understand and blend with one's nation, the universe and, finally, the cosmos. During those moments of reflection, one would notice that the seemingly difficult experiences through which one is going would not appear as consuming as they initially did. We must become humble and peaceful having it at the back of our minds that the quantity of our problems is minute compared to the larger occurrences around the world. The things that choke our happiness are very trivial.

ALWAYS ENVISAGE UNPLEASANT RESULTS. DOING THAT MAKES NOTHING A SHOCK

The things that come as surprises arise during the moments we never expected. For instance, the death of a relative, acute sickness or even civil unrest are not things that occur with prior knowledge. A group of soldiers prepares for battle even when the land is at peace. Human beings are capable of preempting and making prior preparations for any form of chaotic event and its consequences. As we wake every morning, we must always keep ourselves abreast of such things as:

"Today I may lose someone I love, face pain or sickness, fail at my goals, lose my job or my home."

From a distance, we must always project such occurrences and picture ourselves as being reasonable and calm in our responses to them. This would ultimately help make arrangements for even the most brutal results and aid one's appreciation of every day that is filled with positivity.

Prepare for hardship. That way, you won't be depressed or oppressed by any situation. Seneca happened to be one of the richest individuals in Rome. However, he did separate some days during which he lived and acted like he was impoverished. He would hardly eat and he would wear tattered clothes. Seneca practiced this sort of lifestyle to build his body and mind, as well as to keep himself aware that genuine happiness is not the result of external possessions like money or houses.

Just as he did, we can build up our minds by placing ourselves in unpleasant conditions at separate intervals – for instance, taking one's bath with cold water in cold weather, consuming only rice for a whole day, trying to pass the night on a bare floor, or trekking through the streets barefoot. As we do this, we do not merely prepare for the probability of difficult and stressful situations; we understand that those things of which one is particularly scared – commotions and penury – can be managed.

TRAIN TO LIVE ON SMALL PROVISIONS. DESIRE THE THINGS ALREADY IN YOUR POSSESSION

Is it not striking and amusing that the billionaires Mark Zuckerberg and the late Steve Jobs always put on the same set of clothes every single day? It is very certain that they could purchase as many other clothes as they wanted and even have custom-made clothing. They decided to wear the same outfit because that relieved them of difficulties of choice and afforded them more time to face and accomplish other daily targets.

Simplicity is an ideal practice. As time passes, we become used to the activities that go on in our lives and, subsequently, our emotions are detached from them. There is the need to employ simplicity in one's dealings periodically. One can decide to move from one place to another without a personal vehicle for about a week or more. We should also try to ignore some not-so-important engagements and wait to see whether we would not be as elated as we used to be. It is important to keep reminding oneself that one's joy is not derived from physical possessions. When one's expectation is restructured, one instantly realizes how lucky one has been.

ASSUME THAT PHYSICAL OR OUTWARD THINGS ARE NOT PERMANENT POSSESSIONS. THEY WOULD SUBSEQUENTLY BE TAKEN BACK

The only true possession of any human is his or her personal mind. One's physical acquisitions and relations are only temporary blessings that can be retrieved at random. All the human beings with whom one has been in contact will eventually become extinct. One's material possessions may be suddenly destroyed. While it is good to be merry with one's relations at the moment, we should not become excessively attached. External things should be likened to an actor's costume, which will last only as long as the play and be relinquished at the end.

This understanding would assist us in getting the best of those who genuinely love us, rather than having regrets that we were not able to fully extend our appreciating of them. Don't be deceived by common opinions about death. Human beings fear nothing like they fear death. However, Stoicism dictates that nursing fear is largely unreasonable as it is a mere rumor that living beings spread to create panic. Death should be seen as it is – the position we were in before we were born. It is the position to which every human will return just as a voyager would return from a breathtaking voyage. Death completes life's cycle, and the only harsh thing about the phenomenon is the fact that it occurs randomly. A pretty young lad faces the same risk as that faced by an older individual. Death must be preconceived in one's mind with the knowledge that it will occur at a random time. Ultimately, the noblest thing about life is living a fulfilling and happy one – long or short.

GET THE BEST OF A DIFFICULT OR AN UNLUCKY SITUATION AND USE IT TO YOUR ADVANTAGE

Difficulties produce success. Many humans perceive difficulties as devilish – stumbling blocks that deny them the chance to actualize their plans, aims, and profound joy. One should turn this notion around and begin to understand that to test one's might and doggedness, one needs these unpleasant occurrences. In the same way, an athlete gets in contact with challenges on the field. One should use such challenges to assess one's virtuousness and examine one's level of determination. It is one thing to theorize some principles; it is another to correctly put them into practice. Combating hardships is the way to brace one's decisions.

CREATE EQUILIBRIUM FOR YOUR PERCEPTIONS. DISTINGUISH AND DIFFERENTIATE SITUATIONS THROUGH THEIR DISTINCTIVE FEATURES

On many occasions, we find ourselves in positions in which we are depressed or suppressed by external occurrences. We let these things take over our actions. The Stoic preached that bringing an outward event into a particular context and making comparisons with the ways in which such events could be more unpleasant would eventually restructure one's perceptions concerning them.

For instance, one may get annoyed because of a long line at a store. However, remembering that some other countries have supplies in annoyingly short supply, or not at all, would make one sensitive to how especially lucky one is. Before one condemns a minor sickness, one must remember those who have been infected by deadly diseases or put into slavery and dehumanizing circumstances. We should always project each event at its actual size with the consciousness that the irritation or anger that is felt will be neutralized in the end. In addition, one should consider humorous the attention one has placed on very trivial things.

OCCURRENCES ARE NOT THE CAUSE OF YOUR FRUSTRATIONS, YOUR EXPECTATIONS ARE

The world might appear to have been plagued with a series of injustices, vague promises, turndowns, and other vices. Instead of blaming others whenever we are discouraged by all these things, we must find the reasons within one's mind. For instance, if our employer has offended us, what is the reason for our anger? Would it be because we were maltreated or because we believed he or she could not afford to act that way? What informed our opinion that a particular individual or group of individuals would not act wrongly toward us at any point? We should always be conscious of the fact that all disappointments and letdowns emanate from our personal irrational or unachievable expectations for which we are, in fact, responsible. It is never advisable to expect many things, and there should be no form of complaint if the universe decides to operate in a way that is contrary to one's expectations.

SUPPRESS ILLNESS AND PAINS. THEY ARE AVENUES TO SHOWCASE BRAVERY

When confronted with physical illness, we should not be vulnerable to our weaknesses and flaws; indulging in such practices would only lead to further difficulties. We should be conscious of the fact that our illnesses are grounds upon which our claims of virtuousness and determination will be put to the test. We should be a source of inspiration to other humans through our strengths and actions. Courage is imbibed with very few gestures from others – for instance, a situation in which we witness an individual struggling to endure those things that other humans are equally prone to witness.

ALWAYS REMEMBER THAT EVERYTHING IS FAMILIAR. THERE ISN'T REALLY ANYTHING NEW UNDER THE SUN

One can easily conclude that all the unpleasant situations in the world do not happen evenly. Those things have been consistently static since their inception. Two early Stoics who encountered the problems with which we try to battle every day are Seneca and Marcus Aurelius. They also had to confront disease, wars, disasters, dictatorial governments, and many other constraints. Their triumph implies that we should always do away with depression or fear whenever we encounter a challenge. We must always remember that all events have been experienced before. The only difference is the place and participants.

BE PASSIONATE ABOUT HUMANS IN GENERAL. EVERYONE IS INVOLVED

All around the world, human beings have an innate tendency to bond without any fuss. Everyone has had to deal with the pain of losing someone dear. Even then, almost all human beings have fallen to lust, unnecessary anger, and temptations. More than we allow our minds to process, we all have similar experiences in life. Whenever one communicates or encounters colleagues, friends, or relations, it is necessary to be respectable and attentive to their needs and wants. We should always be more concerned about our present dealings as it would subsequently aid in fostering the level of the relationships and increasing one's admiration and regard for other humans.

LEARN TO OVERLOOK THE LAPSES OF OTHERS. EVERYONE ACTS IN LINE WITH THE THINGS THEY KNOW

It is impossible to rule over the inappropriate actions of other humans. We can only manage our personal reactions or responses. If anyone has wronged us, the perpetrators must have done so consciously or unconsciously. Should it have been an unconscious act, it is important that one is not moved or perturbed by his or her ignorance. On the other hand, if he or she carried out the act consciously, one must understand that such an individual has shortcomings in his or her character. It is not within our capacity to provide solutions to such conditions. In his Meditation, Marcus Aurelius expressly stated, *"We can hold our breath until our faces turn blue, yet people will never stop erring."*

ALL ENVIES SHOULD BE NEUTRALIZED WITH GOOD REASONS. ONE CAN ONLY BE SATISFIED THROUGH AN INWARD CONVICTION

As humans, we are ultimately owned by the things we acquire as possessions. Genuine happiness lies within oneself and is not in any way determined by other individuals. Envying what others own and have achieved would not amount to any positive outcome. Everyone is single-handedly responsible for the creation and actualization of his or her happiness. The fact remains that those things one tends to envy are not things that would permanently reside with those who are currently in its possession.

MOTIVATE OTHERS BY ACTING. MERE WORDS MAY BE LARGELY UNPRODUCTIVE

If we wish for others to take after us, we must put our principles into practice. Even without one's knowledge, other people watch one's acts and habits and the way one confronts life's obstacles. Instead of giving instructions to other human beings about how to manage and control harsh situations in the world, these should be demonstrated through actual acts. Epictetus once said, *"We must act not as a sheep who throws up her grass before digesting. Instead, we should act as one who digests her food, thus producing healthy wool and rich milk."*

We are not so different from those with whom we interact. We should be sensible in choosing those to whom we move toward. One's friend shapes one as much as one equally informs their acts.

NEVER FORGET YOUR ROLES AS A HUMAN. LIVE ACCORDING TO THE DICTATES OF NATURE

It is not ideal to do without the natural things the body needs. Sleeping and feeding are necessary to help maintain one's health and life in general. However, we must take a step further. As human beings, we can also reason. It is only natural that we constantly task our rationality. We must use our rational capabilities to ascertain that our thinking and practices reflect virtuousness and are knowledgeable. The ability to stand tall and strive to improve others is a blessing.

YOUR ACTIONS SHOULD NOT BE CARRIED OUT RANDOMLY. TOMORROW HAS NO CERTAINTY

A constant phenomenon in the world is that what happens in some moments after the present is largely unpredictable and not assumable. Still, many humans use their days to move about without a specific aim, purpose, or target.

We must focus our attention on the things that require urgency. Once we have set some goals, we must completely focus and direct all our actions toward achieving them. One should endeavor to get the maximum advantage out of every situation and chance because it is not completely certain that one would have the opportunity to progress with one's plans the day after. The knowledge that death is inevitable should be used as a form of motivation in one's dealings. Through that consciousness, one could always make advancements.

IGNORE UNNECESSARY ATTACHMENTS. FILTERING OUT EXCESSES STRENGTHENS WHAT REMAINS

Focus is a very important habit to cultivate. Ignoring the extras and paying attention to the things that would help shape the course of events in the universe will make one a force to be reckoned with. We must employ all our resources when carrying out those things that time permits. There is no use spending a lot of time on trivial issues. Once we master this habit, there is no limit to what we can achieve during a short period of time. When making decisions about the points to which one's attention should be shifted, Seneca advised, *"You must always be capable of completing the task at hand – stronger than the weight you hope to carry."*

DO NOT ALWAYS ANTICIPATE RICHES AND POPULARITY. REWARDS SHOULD ALWAYS COME AS A SURPRISE

It is not ideal to always anticipate riches. Rather, one's attention should focus on current activities, keeping in mind that the result of one's participation is beyond one's control. Have circumstances placed another person's works above one's own? We must understand that our works would eventually speak for us. As a matter of fact, what is fame? Marcus Aurelius stressed, *"The desire to be admired by future generations is as foolish as hoping you will be admired by your own great-grandfather. Do not expect fame – instead, work to help and enrich the lives of those whose time here you share."*

BE MODERATE IN ALL YOUR DEALINGS; THERE IS PEACE IN LIVING A BALANCED LIFE

Living a moderate life fosters tranquility. It is then important to always act moderately, opt for important things, and completely ignore an elaborate lifestyle. We should always appear as individuals who place value on mankind and not in superfluous living. We should eat only to neutralize hunger, not to indulge in every edible substance. Upon achieving a moderate lifestyle, one can withstand the unpleasant waves of nature. Once-virtuous stances and possessions would not wither at those moments.

THE EVENTS OF THE PAST SHOULD NOT BE A YARDSTICK FOR YOUR CURRENT HABITS. EMPIRICAL FACTS SHOULD BE SOURCED

We are too fond of letting ancient beliefs and practices dictate the ways in which we act. Is it not worrisome that we entrust our lives to the principles of individuals who have existed before us and not one another? We should endeavor to find the truth behind every situation. We should acknowledge that those who existed before us are masters, but are at the same time mere humans too. The fact that a noble individual has behaved in a certain way does not imply that this behavior reflects the best virtue practice. As virtuous as Seneca is assumed to have been, he practiced slavery. Should this be what we practice too? We must reflect on our decisions in the past and remind ourselves that one may later find one's current actions wrong in the future and at a point, one's acts would be recorded as part of one's history. It is important to project humility, exercise courage, and practice virtuousness. We must constantly seek the truth and understand it comprehensively.

CHAPTER 13: Principles for Developing an Unbendable Mind

This chapter is a compilation of notable quotes by reputable Stoics. Being a fervent Stoic requires learning, understanding, and putting these expressions into practice. Here they are:

"You have power over your mind – not outside events. Realize this, and you will find strength." – Marcus Aurelius, Meditations.

"Wealth consists not in having great possessions, but in having few wants." – Epictetus.

"Do not indulge in dreams of having what you have not, but reckon up the chief of the blessings you do possess, and then thankfully remember how you would crave for them if they were not yours." – Marcus Aurelius, Meditations.

"A man thus grounded must, whether he wills or not, necessarily be attended by constant cheerfulness and a joy that is deep and issues from deep within, since he finds delight in his own resources, and desires no joys greater than his inner joys." – Seneca, The Stoic Philosophy of Seneca.

"Don't explain your philosophy. Embody it." – Epictetus.

"The chief task in life is simply this: to identify and separate matters so that I can say clearly to myself which are externals not under my control, and which have to do with the choices I actually control." – Epictetus.

"You are afraid of dying. However, come now, how is this life of yours anything but death?" – Seneca.

"Think of those who, not by fault of inconsistency but by lack of effort, are too unstable to live as they wish, but only live as they have begun." – Seneca

"In all things, we should try to make ourselves be as grateful as possible." – Seneca to Lucilius.

"You can bind up my leg, but not even Zeus has the power to break my freedom of choice." – Epictetus

"I can teach you a love potion made without any drugs, herbs, or special spell – if you would be loved, love." – Hecato.

"In the end, the love you take is equal to the love you make." – The Beatles.

"The mind must be given relaxation – it will rise improved and sharper after a good break." – Seneca, On Tranquility of Mind.

"Dig deep within yourself, for there is a fountain of goodness ever ready to flow if you will keep digging." –

Marcus Aurelius.

"For what can even the most malicious person do if you keep showing kindness and if, given the chance, you gently point out where they went wrong—right as they are trying to harm you?" – Marcus Aurelius.

"Think of the whole universe of matter and how small your share." – Marcus Aurelius.

"Don't behave as if you are destined to live forever. What's fated hangs over you. As long as you live and while you can, become good now." – Marcus Aurelius.

"Let philosophy scrape off your own faults, rather than be a way to rail against the faults of others" – Seneca.

"Often injustice lies in what you aren't doing, not only in what you are doing." - Marcus Aurelius.

"Don't seek for everything to happen as you wish it would, but rather wish that everything happens as it actually will – then your life will flow well." – Epictetus.

"Better to trip with the feet than with the tongue." – Zeno.

"Inwardly, we ought to be different in every respect, but our outward dress should blend in with the crowd." – Seneca.

"It is only ideas gained from walking that have any worth." – Nietzsche.

"We should take wandering outdoor walks so that the

mind might be nourished and refreshed by the open air and deep breathing." – Seneca.

"Don't be ashamed of needing help. You have a duty to fulfill just like a soldier on the wall of battle. So what if you are injured and can't climb up without another soldier's help?" – Marcus Aurelius.

"Watch the stars in their courses and imagine yourself running alongside them." – Marcus Aurelius.

"As each day arises, welcome it as the very best day of all, and make it your own possession. We must seize what flees." – Seneca.

"Believe in yourself and trust that you are on the right path, and not be in doubt by following the myriad footpaths of those wandering in every direction." – Seneca.

"Let each thing you would do, say or intend be like that of a dying person." – Marcus Aurelius.

"Without a ruler to do it against, you can't make crooked straight." – Seneca.

"This is the mark of perfection of character – to spend each day as if it were your last, without frenzy, laziness, or any pretending." – Marcus Aurelius

"Don't set your heart on so many things." – Epictetus.

"The art of living is more like wrestling than dancing because an artful life requires being prepared to meet and withstand sudden and unexpected attacks." – Marcus Aurelius.

"It is impossible for a person to begin to learn what he thinks he already knows." – Epictetus.

"Receive without pride, let go without attachment." – Marcus Aurelius.

"Apply yourself to thinking through difficulties – hard times can be softened, tight squeezes widened, and heavy loads made lighter for those who can apply the right pressure." – Seneca.

"If anyone would take two words to heart and take pains to govern and watch over themselves by them, they will live an impeccable and immensely tranquil life. The two words are: persist and resist." – Epictetus.

"I say, let no one rob me of a single day who isn't going to make a full return on the loss." – Seneca.

"Both Alexander the Great and his mule-keeper were both brought to the same place by death." – Marcus Aurelius.

"Rejoice in all successes and be moved by every failure." – Seneca.

CONCLUSION

Thank you again for purchasing this book!

I hope this book was able to help you learn more about Stoicism.

Finally, if you enjoyed this book, then I'd like to ask you for a favor. Would you be kind enough to leave a review of this book on Amazon? It'd be greatly appreciated!

Made in the USA
San Bernardino, CA
07 March 2018